God is a Symbol of Something True

Why you don't have to choose either a literal creator God or a blind, indifferent universe

First published by O Books, 2009
O Books is an imprint of John Hunt Publishing Ltd., The Bothy, Deershot Lodge, Park Lane, Ropley,
Hants, SO24 0BE, UK
office1@o-books.net
www.o-books.net

Distribution in:

UK and Europe
Orca Book Services
orders@orcabookservices.co.uk
Tel: 01202 665432 Fax: 01202 666219
Int. code (44)

USA and Canada
NBN
custserv@nbnbooks.com
Tel: 1 800 462 6420 Fax: 1 800 338 4550

Australia and New Zealand
Brumby Books
sales@brumbybooks.com.au
Tel: 61 3 9761 5535 Fax: 61 3 9761 7095

Far East (offices in Singapore, Thailand,
Hong Kong, Taiwan)
Pansing Distribution Pte Ltd
kemal@pansing.com
Tel: 65 6319 9939 Fax: 65 6462 5761

South Africa
Alternative Books
altbook@peterhyde.co.za
Tel: 021 555 4027 Fax: 021 447 1430

Text copyright Jack Call 2008

Design: Stuart Davies

ISBN: 978 1 84694 244 0

A CIP catalogue record for this book is available
from the British Library.

Printed by Digital Book Print

O Books operates a distinctive and ethical publishing philosophy in
all areas of its business, from its global network of authors to
production and worldwide distribution.
This book is produced on FSC certified stock, within ISO14001
standards. The printer plants sufficient trees each year through
the Woodland Trust to absorb the level of emitted carbon in
its production.

God is a Symbol of Something True

Why you don't have to choose
either a literal creator God
or a blind, indifferent universe

Jack Call

BOOKS

Winchester, UK
Washington, USA

CONTENTS

Preface

To my sense, "bread" is as inadequate a translation of the human intensity of the Spanish "pan" as "Dios" is of the awful mystery of the English "God." This latter word does not designate an object at all, but a sentiment, a psychosis, not to say a whole chapter of religious history.

George Santayana[1]

When I was very young, and my parents and other grown-ups told me about God the Father and Jesus, it didn't occur to me to ask myself, 'But is it true?' Aware of my own ignorance and dependence, like any young child, I readily accepted the authority of the grown-ups in all cases that didn't frustrate my desires. I had already learned, too, that even when the orders from above did go against my will, it was generally better to obey than to rebel. But the talk about God and His love for us and the stories about Jesus didn't go against any preconceived ideas I had about the nature of reality anyway. They just seemed like facts similar to the facts I was told about animals and plants and the name of our country and who our relatives were. Not only was it unthinkable that my parents would lie to me, I didn't even yet have any reason to think they might be mistaken about anything.

Later on, I discovered that there were some reasons to think the grown-ups, including my parents, might be wrong about some things. After all, they didn't always agree with each other. And it became clear that sometimes grown-ups, just like kids, would lie in order to get out of trouble. So it became quite reasonable to ask myself, about some things I was told, 'But is it true?'

It wasn't until I was fourteen years old, though, that, prodded by a friend, I dared to ask this question about my religious beliefs. Right away it became clear to me that I did not really believe there could be a devil who was trying to capture my soul and take me to Hell. It didn't really make sense to me that God is like a loving Father but that He would willingly let some of His children go to an eternal punishment for not being good enough or for not believing in Him. Suddenly, to my surprise, I realized that I didn't believe in God at all! I had believed, or thought I believed, that God existed and that those who believed in Him and asked forgiveness for their sins would be rewarded eternally and that those who didn't believe in Him, and who were too proud to ask for forgiveness or who didn't realize they were sinners, would be eternally punished. But now that I had rejected the punishment part, it seemed clear that there was no justification for the reward part either. But this in a way was its own reward. I felt liberated, as if a weight had been lifted from my shoulders. It suddenly seemed so clear to me. God was supposed to be in Heaven, but it was admitted that Heaven wasn't literally up above, somewhere in outer space. People talked about God a lot, and as I learned in Sunday School, in the old days God had supposedly talked to certain people, too. But no one claimed any more that God literally talked to them that way, or if they did, we dismissed them as either fakes or crazy people. God was nowhere to be seen or heard, and, as far as I could see, the belief that He existed didn't really help explain anything. It seemed as if religious believers were all just pretending that something was true that they wanted to be true, which is why they hated anyone who would dare to call it into doubt.

Since that time I've had many other intellectual and emotional adventures, which have had the effect of complicating and deepening my thoughts and feelings about religion. A few years after my atheistic epiphany, I discovered the writings of the French existentialist philosopher Albert Camus, an atheist who found meaning in the brave confrontation with an indifferent universe and who embraced the absurdity of the human condition. I supposed, then, that I was an existentialist, although

I was none too clear about the meaning of Sartre's slogan that existence precedes essence. I took my first philosophy class in college and was delighted to find a setting where it was always all right to ask, 'But is it true?' Then, with surprising suddenness, the controversy over the use of LSD and similar substances was abroad in the land, and I developed an intense interest in religious experiences and the writings of mystics. My new intellectual heroes were the novelist Aldous Huxley, who popularized the term "psychedelic" (mind-manifesting) and proposed a religious interpretation of psychedelic experience, and Alan Watts, the former Anglican priest and eloquent interpreter of Hinduism, Taoism, and Buddhism (especially the Zen variety). Before long, I joined a psychedelic church and devoted myself to it for a number of years, until I eventually became as disillusioned with that church as I had earlier been with the church of my childhood. Now a secular humanist, I turned back to the study of philosophy, which had been my major as an undergraduate. There followed a longer, calmer period of development, raising a family, learning a profession. And now I find myself once again fascinated by religion. So it has been, back and forth, from a pro to a con attitude towards religion, back to a pro, back to a con, and now again back to a pro attitude. But rather than a simple back and forth motion, I think of intellectual and spiritual development as a spiral. When one comes back again to the earlier point, it isn't exactly the same point, but is one level further out, or in, depending on which sounds better to you. The upshot is that I'm now a professional philosopher who has been teaching philosophy at the "retail level" (community college) for the past fifteen years. When I first starting teaching the Introduction to Philosophy class, I avoided philosophy of religion as much as I could, because I thought of religion as a rival to philosophy. It was dogmatism versus open inquiry. But I have found that, for better or worse, religion has played such an important role in the lives of my students, as it has in mine, that it is folly to try to avoid it and to concentrate on other branches of philosophy. So, I devote a considerable portion of the semester to philosophy of religion. In addition to the question, 'But is it true?' always encouraged in a philosophy class, there is another one, entwined with it, that applies especially to any philosophical or religious view: 'What does it mean?' That is the question I am at long last asking about the Biblical account of God and trying to answer in this book.

This is a book of philosophy of religion, but it is also the expression of a particular religious view, something which I would avoid imposing on a captive audience of college students, but which I offer to members of the reading public who are free to read it or not. It is not a textbook, not a survey of world religions, not a scholarly treatise on the topic of religion (although I aim to meet scholarly standards). Rather, it is an articulation of a view that, as the subtitle indicates, rejects the false dilemma of choosing between a literal acceptance of theistic dogma, on the one hand, and scientism, i.e., the worship of science, on the other. I expect it will appeal most to those who, like me, were raised as Christians of the Protestant persuasion, who are no longer believers in any traditional sense, but who appreciate the great artistic and intellectual achievements of Christian civilization, and want to make sense of religious and moral concepts in a way that is true to their deepest experiences. It may be that this view is a true version of Christianity, but I would not insist on it. I'm convinced that it is true religion, whatever other label is informative. Maybe it is best just to call it "individualistic religion." Of course, I hope that people who were raised in other traditions will also find here a view that is compatible with their deepest experiences, but I can't hope to do justice to the particular nuances that being raised in a different tradition would impart to one's worldview.

The central claim of this book is that everything is fundamentally all right, in spite or because of the fact that there are important things that one cares about deeply, over which one has no control and never will. What makes this book unique is the claim that God is a symbol of that fact and that this gives us a new way to understand the Biblical tradition, morality, and the human condition. Of course, these are controversial claims, and that is why I try to explain and support them at some length and in some detail. My fondest hope for this book is that it will find readers who, having read it, will feel that they are better people for having done so.

Personal Thanks

The love and bedrock decency of my mother, Clare Call, and my late father, Cleo Call, are gifts that I can only accept gracefully and try to emulate. My brother John and my sister Shirley are also important influences in my life. My wife, Mary Jo, is a spiritual and physical treasure. My two sons, Stan and Aaron; my daughter-in-law, Ronnette; and my two grandchildren, Nick and Clare, have enriched my life immeasurably. Aaron's careful reading and notes identified passages that needed clarification. Mary Jo's proofreading and questions helped make this a better book, and Stan's words of encouragement spurred me on. Comments from my old friend, Roark Hunnicutt, and my colleague and friend, Rudy Saldana, were also helpful. The students in the classes I have taught over the years have helped me more than they might imagine. My teaching methods have changed, and so has my thinking, in response to my interactions with them. I wrote this book while on sabbatical leave from Citrus College. I am grateful to the sabbatical committee for recommending my proposal and to the Board of Trustees for approving it. Finally, my publisher, O Books, is a writer's dream of what a publisher should be like. I welcome feedback from readers. You may e-mail me at jckcall@yahoo.com.

Jack Call
Whittier, California
10 October 2008

Chapter 1

Individualistic Religion

What is religion, and is there a true one?

Everyone departs life as if he or she had only just been born.

Epicurus[2]

Is there such a thing as a true religion? Much blood has been and is still being spilled over this question. Among civilized people, many would agree in answering, 'Yes,' and agree to disagree about which one it is. Others would answer, 'No. Religion is a snare and a delusion.' Others would answer, 'I don't know. It is possible, but there is no way we can know for sure.'

Let's be clear that the question is not whether there is any truth in any religion. Even someone who thinks that religion on the whole is a bad thing that we would all be better off without will generally concede that there are some true propositions among those that constitute the point of view of many religious people. For example, some version of the Golden Rule is espoused in most religious views, and an atheist doesn't need to reject this fundamental principle of morality in order to reject belief in God and other supernatural beings. No, the question is: Is there a religion that on the whole tells the truth about whatever religion is about? This question leaves it open that there could be more than one, since there can be more than one way of telling the truth, but at least it isn't so open-ended that even someone who thinks religion is a delusion can also answer, 'Yes.'

I'm going to defend a "Yes" answer to this question, but right away I need to tell you that I'm not going to be able to tell you, by name, which one it is (or which ones). This is not because I'm being coy or diplomatic. No, quite the contrary, I fear. I want to

1

defend what I take to be the true religion, as well as I can make out, but the only label for it that seems accurate is to call it individualistic religion. By this I mean that a person's salvation consists in realizing that everything is fundamentally all right, and that no one can have this realization for you. Religious faith is living up to this realization. Sin is not living up to it, and is a matter of degree. Damnation is living a life that makes the world worse.

Two big objections spring to mind. One is that, despite my use of Christian terminology ("salvation," "faith," "sin"), there is nothing particularly religious about what I've said. It sounds like just a "philosophy of life" to say that everything is fundamentally all right, and a pretty shallow one at that, which is the second objection. Everything is not fundamentally all right. How can anyone with a conscience complacently say that everything is fundamentally all right while people suffer terrible accidents or get old and sick and die and while some people do horrible things to others? I'll answer the second objection first and then get back to the first one.

The claim that everything is fundamentally all right doesn't imply that there is no room for improvement, or that this is the best of all possible worlds. A god-like intelligence would be necessary in order to know whether or not this is the best of all possible worlds, but it is not required in order to realize that everything is fundamentally all right. It is all right even if it isn't the best. It is very easy to imagine innumerable ways in which it could be improved. No one should be complacent. Everyone should do whatever he or she can to make things better. The realization that everything is fundamentally all right doesn't imply that there is an omniscient, omnipotent, benevolent God who makes sure that nothing goes wrong. The problem of evil is a devastating objection to that claim. The problem of learning how to retain faith that everything is fundamentally all right while acknowledging evil, is a problem for every philosophy of life, whether religious or non-religious, or so I shall argue; and I don't even claim to be particularly good at it. I also freely confess that this is merely a verbal formula for expressing something, a realization, that I am not presently having in the deepest sense.

As for my use of Christian terminology ("salvation," "faith," "sin") while declining to identify as a Christian, I suppose that, in one sense, I could call myself a Christian, just as the late Italian journalist, Oriana Fallaci, called herself a Christian atheist because she preferred Christian civilization to any other. However, that is certainly not a sense that is going to satisfy an evangelical Christian interested in getting me to save my immortal soul from hellfire by accepting Jesus Christ as my personal savior. I don't literally believe in God or personal immortality. I am much attracted to the vagueness of Taoism. However, the narrative and insistently personal aspects of Judaism and Christianity are fascinating and hit on something essential to individualistic religion. (This is probably true of Islam also, but I am much less familiar with that religion.) I think it is salvation and faith that I am interested in.

In order to answer the objection that there isn't anything particularly religious in just saying that everything is fundamentally all right, I need to address the question contained within the question: Is there a religion that on the whole tells the truth about whatever religion is about? That is, what is religion about; or, what makes something a religion; or, what is the essence of religion? I claim that religion has to do with how we think and feel about the fact that we are not in control of some of the things in life that are most important to us. This characterization doesn't imply that religion is theistic, although it is consistent with the popularity of theism. 'After all,' the theist might say, 'if we aren't in control, then someone else is, and that someone else must be more powerful and wise than we humans are. Otherwise, we would be in control.' But my claim about the essence of religion is also consistent with atheism, that is, the view that it isn't a "someone" else, but just a "something" else that limits our control, and that things, unlike persons, are neither wise nor unwise.

This characterization of religion does imply that a scientist's motivation, whether he or she is a theist or an atheist, may be a religious motivation. The goal of science is to attain the kind of understanding that increases our powers of prediction and control, consistently with an understanding of how things got to be the way they are. Trying to achieve that goal is one way of responding to the fact that there are important things about which we are ignorant. Still, there is a distinction between religion and science that cannot be blurred. Science is the kind of knowledge that gives us more control or at least points the way to what would be required in order to have more control. Religion confronts the fact that no matter how much scientific knowledge we have, there are things that we care about that we can't control. Religion is essentially emotional and subjective in a way that science is not. It is about how we think *and feel* about not being in control. That is why religion can motivate a scientist but cannot be scientific. Scientists, like all human beings, feel emotions and have a subjective point of view, but the goal of science is to exclude these subjective considerations as much as possible so as to approach an objective point of view that is accessible from the subjective point of view of everyone willing and able to do the work required to understand it and to put aside any emotional baggage that conflicts with it.

Although religion, unlike science, does not require one to put aside emotions and subjectivity, it doesn't follow that religion makes no claim to objective truth. When a religious person believes, for example, that a certain thing is beyond his or her control, he or she believes this to be objectively true. What makes the point of view religious is that it goes beyond the mere claim that something is not within one's power, to include an emotional response to that belief. As I've indicated, in what I believe to be

4

the true religion, as in the religions I am most familiar with, that emotional response may be characterized as serene acceptance, or surrender, or faith. However, the opposite reaction - rejection, rebellion, or radical skepticism - needs to be contained somehow within that response. When rejection, rebellion, or radical skepticism is the dominant mood, and a person refuses any ultimate reconciliation, this may still be a religious point of view in the very broadest sense. However, I wouldn't want to insist on this, since it would be insulting to someone who simply rejects religion to be told that even her or his rejection is still a religious response. In any case, it isn't science.

In order to further support the claim that true religion is individualistic, it may be helpful to compare and contrast both religion and science with another important branch of human endeavor, politics. The goal of politics is to increase one's control over things by acting in concert with others to control things that a group can control collectively but that an individual cannot control. Commerce has this same goal, but it is restricted to the means of voluntarily trading goods and services, whereas politics includes the use of coercive power as a means. Science, likewise, is a cooperative enterprise that differs from politics by excluding the use of coercive power.

An individual acting alone can't form a club or a monetary system or a nation, and can't effectively defend herself or himself against an organized coercive threat; but individuals acting collectively can. Very few of us have ever made an original scientific discovery, but most of us take for granted a scientific knowledge base that has been painstakingly gained over many generations by those who are curious enough to do the hard work and thinking required to make scientific progress. We are each of us, as individuals, the beneficiaries of a tremendous wealth of economic and cultural goods passed down to us from preceding generations and protected by collective security arrangements. I hope it is clear then, that in arguing that true religion is individualistic, I am not simply ignoring the benefits, and necessity for human well-being, of society.

Although ideally, in principle, there need be no conflict between religion and science, or between religion and politics, or between science and politics, it is easy to see how there can be in practice. Between religion and science conflict often arises when a false religious belief that something is beyond one's control delays the use of the scientific method to bring that thing under our predictive understanding and control after all. There can also be a religious or quasi-religious enthusiasm for science, i.e. scientism, that unrealistically sees science as ultimately, in principle, bringing everything important under our control, and this thwarts true religion. Between religion and politics, one well-known conflict is the one over whether religious acceptance isn't just a palliative for political oppression, as in Marx's critique of religion.[3] Another conflict between religion and politics that is more dangerous for true religion is when religious people think they are furthering their religion by gaining more political control in the name of it, or when politics becomes a substitute for religion. If I am right that the goal of religion is to confront the fact that there are things - and very important things - that are not under our control, either individually or collectively, then neither gaining scientific knowledge nor political power can further the goal of religion. False religion is religion that tries to take the place of science or politics. False science and false politics each try to take the place of religion. True religion is individualistic in that anyone else's religious salvation is irrelevant to your own existential anxiety. In contrast, most of our powers of predictive control are gained in cooperation with other people. It is also possible to benefit from being subject to the coercive powers of the state that are collectively created and enforced, but it is not possible either to coerce or to be coerced into realizing that everything is fundamentally all right.

Why is this a religion, though, and not just a philosophy? The goal of philosophy is to attain a clear and comprehensive conceptual framework for assessing the problems of life and the most promising solutions to them. What I am doing here, for instance, is trying to construct a conceptual framework of the relations between science, religion, politics, and philosophy itself. This is philosophy, but my subject matter is, mainly, religion. What distinguishes philosophy and religion, on this understanding, is that religion essentially includes an emotional response that is not essential to philosophy. When philosophy does include it, there is only this conceptual distinction between the two: that we might still call it "philosophy" either with or without that emotional response, but it wouldn't be religion without it.

An interesting application of this distinction, which will help support my claim that my subject is true religion, is to consider whether we should classify the teachings of the ancient Greek philosopher Epicurus as philosophy, as is usually done, or as religion. Epicurus himself wrote of the necessity of becoming a natural philosopher, i.e. a scientist, in order to overcome the anxieties fostered by false religion. He taught that everything that exists is either an eternally existing material atom, or a conglomeration of such atoms, or empty space. He said that it is clear that the gods exist, since we have distinct knowledge of them, and that the correct conception of a god is of a naturally immortal and perfectly blessed being who would have no trouble in mind or body and so would have no reason to cause us any trouble either.[4] On this view, a god would be a material being, presumably an eternally existing conglomeration of atoms, since it is hard to see how a single atom could be blessed. A god would not be a creator of the universe. The universe has always existed and always will. So, Epicurus is not even a deist, much less a theist in the sense of someone who believes in a God who not only created but also sustains the universe. It doesn't seem quite right to call him an atheist either, in the sense of someone who denies the existence of any god. But all that is irrelevant if I am right that the mark of religion is an emotional response to the fact there are important things over which we have no control. For that is what Epicurus' teaching is all about. He wrote that some things occur by necessity, some things occur by chance, and there are some things that are within our control. We can do nothing about those things that occur by necessity, we should view the things that occur by chance as opportunities, and we should see that the remaining things over which we do have control are sufficient for ensuring that we can have lives that approach the blessedness of the gods.

One of the more enigmatic sayings attributed to Epicurus is the one I placed at the head of this chapter: 'Everyone departs life as if he or she had only just been born.' It is clear that Epicurus taught that, when it comes to what really matters - our happiness - we are not helpless. All that is required is for us to become philosophers, cultivate friendship, cease cultivating vain desires, and realize that it is easy to fulfill the natural, necessary desires, that acute suffering never lasts and that chronic suffering is outweighed by what can still be enjoyed in life, and that death is no more fearful than the state we were in before we were born. So, although we do suffer and die, unlike the gods, who do neither, we can approach the blessedness of the gods in our natural happiness. We should not desire to be immortal because this is a vain desire, that is, one that cannot possibly be fulfilled. 'Against all else it is possible to provide security; but as far as death is concerned, we all dwell in an unfortified city.'[5] But what did Epicurus (or one of his followers) mean, when he or she said, 'Everyone departs life as if he or she had only just been born'? Does this mean that it's as if all the experiences of the intervening years had never happened? If so, then this saying would be an expression of despair in the face of existential anxiety about meaninglessness. If, ultimately, it's as if the experiences that we had in life had never happened, then having them in the first place is pointless. However, this would undermine Epicurus' reasoned reassurance against the anxiety about the meaning-lessness of being controlled by some impersonal force, and so it seems unlikely that this is the correct interpretation; for he said that it would be better to believe in the gods of the popular imagi-nation than to believe in the destiny of the natural philosophers, since there is at least hope of successfully placating the gods, while there is no hope against an impersonal force like destiny or an all-encompassing necessity.[6]

An alternative interpretation is that this saying means that we face death as helplessly as a newborn infant. That is, nothing that we could have learned in those intervening years enables us to avoid dying. This is consistent with the claim that the desire for immortality is a vain desire, but it also expresses a tenderness towards that foolish desire which is of questionable consistency with the cold logic of Epicurus' argument against the fear of death: Where we are, death is not; where death is, we are not. Therefore, death is nothing to us.[7]

The tender feeling evoked by the helplessness of an infant and the comparison with our own helplessness at any age, in the face of death, seems to say that death is not nothing to us. It is something that provokes existential anxiety, which is a form of suffering. Of course, Epicurus thought this is unnecessary suffering and that we can overcome it through a correct conception of death. He is right, I think, that when I am dead, I won't know what I'm missing. Subjectively, being dead is not like anything at all. There just won't be any subjective point of view of mine any more. The "experience" of being dead is identical with the "experience" of not yet being born. That is, it is the having of no experience. What is so terrible about that? After all, I don't feel dread at the thought that before I ever had any experiences, countless eons had passed, beginning with the very beginning of time, if time can have a beginning; so why should I feel dread at the thought that some day I will quit having experiences forever and ever? The answer seems to be just that I am oriented toward the future. My previous limitless lack of subjective awareness doesn't bother me because it is over and done with. The cutting off of any further awareness I anticipate at my death is still to come.

Let us suppose, though, that Epicurus' reasoning cures someone of the unnecessary suffering of the dread of death. Will this person leave life as though he or she had just been born? Since it's reasonable to assume that newborns don't dread death, because they have no concept of it; this person will leave life like a newborn in that he or she won't dread death. However, that can't be what Epicurus meant by the saying unless he held that everyone, at some time before dying, gets irreversibly cured of the dread of death. That would be a happy outcome, but it doesn't seem very realistic, and Epicurus promoted realistic happiness.

Suppose a baby is born and then dies a few minutes later. That baby would have died, not "as if" it had just been born, but it really would have died just after being born. In what way are all our lives like that? One way is that our finite lifespans, no matter how long or short, are tiny compared to the immense times before and after them. But a complaint about the brevity of life is inconsistent with Epicurus' teaching that it is the quality and not the quantity of our experiences that counts. Since he thought that freedom from trouble in the mind and in the body is the greatest good, it would make sense for him to hold that a life that lasted ten minutes and one that lasted ninety years could be compared in degrees of blessedness just as fairly as two lives of equal length, simply in terms of the ratio of painful to pain-free existence. However, this interpretation gives rise to the traditional complaint against Epicureanism and every other variety of hedonism: Whether or not a life is meaningful is not synonymous with the question of whether or not it contains a surplus of pleasure over pain. Or, to put it another way, a follower of Epicurus needs to say more about how we can free ourselves of the suffering that takes the form of anxiety about meaninglessness.

'Everyone departs life as if he or she had only just been born.'
So far, I have failed to find an interpretation that is satisfying and
consistent with Epicurus' teachings. For some reason, I find this
saying comforting. So, here is another effort. Maybe it means that,
despite external appearances, life is just as fresh and astonishing
at the end as at the beginning. That is consistent with the rest of
what Epicurus said, for example:

> The flesh considers the limits of pleasure to be boundless, and
> only infinite time makes it possible. But the mind, having
> gained a reasonable understanding of the end and limit of the
> flesh, and having expelled fears about eternity, furnishes the
> complete life, and we no longer have any need for time
> without end. But the mind does not flee from pleasure nor,
> when circumstances bring about the departure from life, does
> it take its leave as though falling short somehow of the best
> life.[8]

There is in this passage, as in most of the writings attributed to
Epicurus or his followers, an emphasis on reason rather than
emotion ("the flesh"), but it isn't that Epicurus recommends a
suppression of the emotions. Rather he advocates an understanding of them. An emotional response comes through in the
following passage, which seems at odds with a cool detachment
in the face of the inevitability of death:

> I have anticipated you, Fortune, and barred your means of
> entry. Neither to you nor to any other circumstances shall we
> hand ourselves over as captives. But when necessity compels
> us, we shall depart from life, spitting on it and on those who
> vainly cling to it, declaring in a beautiful song of triumph how
> well we have lived.[9]

Then he writes in the next passage:

As long as we are on the road (of life), we must make the later journey better than the beginning, but be happy and content when we have reached the end.[10]

Surely this is neither science nor politics. It confronts one of the things that are not subject to our control: our own death. It is more than just a conceptual framework; it includes an emotional response. So, it is a philosophy, but it could also reasonably be classified as a religious point of view. Epicurus is the father of scientism and probably its ablest practitioner.

Chapter 2

Second Thoughts and a Reaffirmation

What should we hope about the beginning and end of life?

> Not only our experiences, but all we have done, whatever great thoughts we may have had, and all we have suffered, all this is not lost, though it is past; we have brought it into being. Having been is also a kind of being, and perhaps the surest kind.
>
> Viktor Frankl[11]

On second thought, maybe it isn't very comforting to think that life is just as fresh and astonishing at the end as at the beginning. Maybe it would be more comforting to think that one gradually or suddenly loses interest in life, just as one gradually or suddenly loses the vigor of youth. That way, one could welcome death as a relief from a burden. For if life is just as fresh and astonishing at the end as at the beginning, then death is a great loss.

Of course we know that Epicurus would explain that death is not a great loss, because (he would say) a great loss has to be a subjective experience and when a person dies he or she no longer has any subjective experiences. However, I don't think we should be satisfied with Epicurus' reasoning on that point. This isn't because a person will continue to have subjective experiences after death. It's just that it seems to me that a great loss does not have to be a subjective experience. One does, I believe, lose any further subjective experiences when one dies, and that is a loss, and a great loss. It is a wonderful thing to be conscious and self-aware.

Nevertheless, we should hope that life is just as fresh and astonishing at the end as at the beginning. We should not hope to lose interest in life gradually or suddenly, so as not to experience death as a loss. Death is a loss. Facing death is facing the absolute and final cutoff of the more or less confident expectation of an indefinitely long future as a conscious, self-aware person among all the others. It is true that that can be a good thing, when a person realistically has nothing to look forward to other than suffering, but even in those cases, death is still the loss of that consciousness that was a necessary condition for whatever made life worthwhile before the onset of the terminal suffering.

So, how can it be fundamentally all right that people we love either have died already or will die in the future, and that we will too? And why should we hope that life will be as precious to us just before we die as it was when we were in the pink of health? It is because we want to experience the emotions of joy and sorrow that accompany a meaningful life, rather than the oscillation between anxiety and dull hopelessness that comes when life seems meaningless. Anxiety about death and anxiety about meaninglessness are connected to each other in the following interesting way. If life is really meaningless, then whether we live or die doesn't matter. But if we're anxious about death, then it does matter to us whether we live or die. It must be that we think that life is meaningful, but that death somehow erases that meaningfulness. But if death can really erase the meaningfulness of life, then for all practical purposes, life isn't meaningful in the first place. This takes us back to the starting point. How can we break out of this circle? It is highly desirable to become convinced that it is fundamentally all right that we are each doomed to die even though life is meaningful and it does matter to us whether we live or die.

Clearly, an appeal to the intellect alone is insufficient, but it is necessary. That it is insufficient is the reason why I noted above that we feel joy and sorrow about things that are meaningful to us.

The times when one feels those emotions provide the necessary emotional proof that life is not meaningless. The joy that comes when everything is going just right requires no further justification and proves that it has all been worth it. The grief we feel when someone we love dies is as true as anything can be. Someone who was there and available for interaction is no longer there in that way. But besides this loss to ourselves we are aware of the loss to the dead person himself or herself, of any more of the joy that life and only life can bring.

An appeal to the intellect is necessary because thinking and feeling inevitably influence each other, as they should. So, we need to think of how to conceive of death. It is logically possible that when, by all objective criteria, a person has died, he or she continues to be subjectively aware, either as a disembodied spirit or with a new body in some other world. However, if that does turn out to be the case, it will still also continue to be possible that there will come a time when, once and for all, he or she really finally dies by becoming permanently unconscious. I shall take up the question of whether or not immortality is desirable in the next chapter. For now, let's deal with facing mortality, by which I mean permanent unconsciousness. Given this understanding of death, it is a loss to the person who dies, not because the person continues to be conscious in some spirit world and longs to be back in this world, but rather because, even though the dead person doesn't know it, he or she is missing something, namely the continued life he or she would be living if death had not cut off that possibility. On this conception of death, it is an objective fact that the dead person no longer has any subjective awareness. How, then, can it be fundamentally all right that people die? It is because there is another objective fact that compensates and more than compensates for this one: the objective fact that this person was born and lived exactly the life he or she lived. We have two objective facts, then, that are both independent of the subjective awareness, or lack of it, of the dead person. One is that he or she

15

has been cut off from the possibility of any more of the joys that life can bring. The other is that she or he did have just that life that she or he had. Death cuts off any future life, but it doesn't go back and erase the life that was already there. Nothing can. It is fundamentally all right that we all inevitably die, not because we will still be conscious in some spirit world that is better than this one, but because our lives in this world were worth living, and death simply has no effect on that fact. So, paradoxically, the only person who should think that it is not fundamentally all right that he or she will die is someone who thinks that his or her life has not been worth living. What explains the paradox is that, for such a person, this wouldn't be because there is something especially bad about death but rather because, whether extended indefinitely or cut short, life would not be worth living and hence everything would most definitely not be all right.

So, now we need to address the question: What makes life worth living? Or, what makes life meaningful? A preliminary question is: What does it mean to say of something that it is meaningful, or that it is meaningless? We have clear examples in spoken and written language. A sound or a shape is either a letter or it isn't, in the context of a spoken or written communication. A string of letters is either a word or not in a particular language. If it is, it can be used in a sentence of that language. A well-constructed sentence is a string of words that has a clear meaning in a specific context. A well-constructed paragraph creates a context for sentences, and has a clear meaning in the context of a literary work. A well-constructed literary work in turn has a clear meaning in the context of human life. It becomes increasingly difficult to specify the rules as we move from what counts as a letter (Is it in the alphabet?); to what counts as a word (Is it in a standard dictionary?), to what qualifies as a well-constructed sentence (Does it have a subject and a verb? Is it a complete thought?), to what qualifies as a well written paragraph (Does it have a topic sentence? Is it about a single topic? Are the sentences arranged so as to make the meaning clear?), to what counts as a well-constructed literary work. There are clear differences between well-constructed literary works and poorly constructed ones, and some of these differences are simply inherited from the lower levels, but there are many considerations in addition to whether or not the work contains spelling, punctuation, and grammatical errors. The purpose of the work in the context of human life has to come into consideration.

This seems to show that the kind of meaning that is clear in simple examples like the difference between a piece of writing (meaningful) and a piece of scribbling (not meaningful) is ultimately dependent on what it was supposed to help explain, namely, the kind of meaning that life itself either has or fails to have; for if life itself is meaningless, then the distinction between writing and scribbling is also meaningless. We shouldn't give up too easily, though. For one thing, looking at simple examples like this can help us see that asking 'What is the meaning of life?' is rather like asking, 'What is the meaning, not just of a particular word or sentence, or even a particular book or poem, but of all of literature?' Words, sentences, paragraphs, literary works are meaningful, but different ones mean different things. Similarly, lives could be meaningful, but different lives could be meaningful in different ways. For another thing, the fact that we find some stories more interesting than others gives some indication of the kind of meaning that a life can have. It has the same kind of meaning that an interesting story has. However, life is not just a story, because it is the thing upon whose meaningfulness stands or falls the interest of any story. Now here comes a surprising twist: the very fact that a person cares whether his or her life is really and truly and ultimately meaningful shows that it is. Anxiety about meaninglessness presupposes the meaningfulness of the question of whether life is meaningful. If life really were meaningless, then it would be meaningless and hence unimportant and hence not an occasion for anxiety that it were meaningless. As Paul Tillich wrote, in *The Courage to Be*, 'Even in the despair about meaning being affirms itself through us.'[12] In short, either it would be a bad thing, or it wouldn't, for life to be meaningless. If you honestly think it wouldn't be a bad thing, then you don't need to worry about suffering the anxiety of meaninglessness. If, on the other hand, you honestly think it would be a bad thing and if you do in fact experience meaninglessness as the ultimate threat at times, then that shows that life is fraught with meaning for you, for this very question of its meaningfulness hangs in the balance. In other words, if it would be a bad thing for life to be meaningless, then it isn't meaningless.

Succinctly stated like that, this sounds like the epitome of wishful thinking, much like asserting that since it is unpleasant to think that one will some day die and never be conscious again, it must be true that one is guaranteed to regain consciousness somehow after death. However, it is a mistake to think that the two cases are alike. It is a matter of logic and not just wishful thinking, that anxiety about meaninglessness presupposes the meaningfulness of life. In contrast, desiring to evade death does not presuppose that one will be able to do so.

This argument should help toward the realization that everything is fundamentally all right. Meaninglessness is a bigger threat than death. Most people, I dare say, would rather die having lived a meaningful life than to achieve immortality at the expense of meaninglessness. It would be very difficult to be convinced of the sincerity of someone who claimed to believe that life is meaningless but who confessed to be deeply worried by the prospect of dying.

Is the meaningfulness of life that is presupposed by anxiety about meaninglessness immune to being wiped out by death? It is so only if it is objectively true that one's life is meaningful, for death is the end of one's own subjective awareness. We have to be very careful here. This is tricky, because anxiety of any sort is a subjective state. So, in particular, is the experience I mentioned above of meaninglessness as the ultimate threat. Realizing that everything is fundamentally all right is also a subjective state. On the other hand, when we say, for example, that anxiety is a subjective state, we are claiming that it is objectively true that anxiety is a subjective state. We aren't saying it is just a matter of taste whether you consider anxiety to be a subjective state. Nor are we saying that it is just a matter of taste whether a person's death is the end of that person's subjective awareness. Someone could argue that we have no way of knowing for sure that death is the end of subjective awareness, short of dying and finding out for ourselves; but even so, it is either true or it isn't that death is the end of one's own subjective awareness. It is important to understand that there are objective facts about subjective states. For example, I am presently feeling a pain in my back. That is a subjective experience, but it is an objective fact that I am having it just now. It is important to understand that there are objective facts about subjective experiences, because death cuts off any future subjective experiences of the person who dies, and it ends the existence of that person's body as a living body, and that is all that it does. Death prevents things from happening that otherwise would have happened, but it can't make what has already happened be as if it hadn't happened. Death cannot somehow make false what is already true, namely that the person who died was alive and did have all the subjective experiences that made up his or her inner life. Therefore, death cannot erase the meaningfulness of life that is presupposed by anxiety about meaninglessness, even though such anxiety is a subjective experience. Neither can it eliminate any of the joys or sorrows that a person has experienced and that constitute the emotional proof that life is meaningful. So, yes, we should hope that life is just as fresh and astonishing at the end as at the beginning.

Chapter 3

The True Religion and Christianity

Do we hope we will be resurrected on Judgment Day?

His disciples said to him, 'When will the kingdom come?'
<Jesus said,> 'It will not come by waiting for it. It will not be a matter of saying "here it is" or "there it is". Rather, the kingdom of the father is spread out upon the earth, and men do not see it.'

The Gospel of Thomas[13]

In Chapter 2 we found a reason to believe that life is meaningful, namely, simply that we care whether or not it is meaningful, and our caring, if nothing else, gives a meaning to life. If we could find an effective reason not to care, then we could consistently believe that life is meaningless and that wouldn't bother us. Personally, I'm not motivated to find such a reason. I want life to be meaningful, and I am willing to pay the price of experiencing occasional episodes of anxiety about meaninglessness. I have faith that I will be able to come out of them.

There is more to be said, of a more positive nature, about tuning in to the meaningfulness of life. I will leave that for a later chapter, though, because I first want to address the question of whether the main points of the discussion so far are consistent with Christianity. I've claimed that the essence of religion is an individual confronting the fact that there are things that really matter but that are outside her or his control. Among these are the identities of one's parents and the circumstances of one's birth and upbringing. These circumstances include the religious beliefs of one's parents and the dominant religious tradition of one's culture. As one grows up one eventually gains control over how one decides to relate to these at any given moment, whether to accept them unquestioningly or to rebel against them or to accept some parts and reject others; but the beliefs and actions of other people that constitute the religious traditions are among those important things that remain outside one's control.

The dominant religious tradition in my culture is Christianity, and my religious upbringing was in the Protestant tradition. There is also a secular tradition in my culture, and I am aware of other religious traditions and have become educated about them to varying degrees. However, although I wouldn't call myself a Christian, for reasons to be explained, I am much more inclined to argue that my views are consistent with what we might call "true Christianity" than I am to argue that they are consistent with "true Judaism," "true Islam," "true Buddhism," or "true Hinduism" or anything else. Weird names from the Old Testament; Sunday School posters and Bible illustrations of men, women, and children in strange garb in a dusty land; choral and organ music and congregational singing; ritualistic verbal formulas; genuine loving kindness alternating with shameless guilt manipulation; Christmas carols: such is the peculiar combination of alternately charming and revolting elements that push my emotional buttons to this day. They probably have their equivalents in other religious traditions; but starting over from childhood with adoptive parents would be required to know those the way I know these, i.e., with a similar depth of emotion. So, I'm not competent to say, really, whether the view I am working out here is consistent with the true version of any religious tradition other than Christianity. On the other hand, since truth transcends all subjective points of view, if there is such a thing as a true Christianity, a true Judaism, a true Islam, a true Buddhism, a true Hinduism, etc., then they will all be simply the true religion.

The question was whether the main points so far are consistent with Christianity. Those main points are: 1) that salvation is the realization that everything is fundamentally all right; 2) that if it would be a bad thing for life to be meaningless, then it isn't meaningless; 3) that death can only prevent things from happening, so it can't wipe out the objective meaningfulness of subjective experiences that have already happened; and 4) from these, that we should hope that life is just as fresh and astonishing at the end as at the beginning.

Arguably, the first claim, that salvation is the realization that everything is fundamentally all right, is consistent with the Christian view that salvation is the forgiveness of sins; since believing that one's sins are forgiven could well be experienced as a realization that everything is fundamentally all right. However, the second and third claims, about the objective meaningfulness of life and its immunity to being wiped out by death, at least seem to be inconsistent with the claim that life would be meaningless unless there is an afterlife in which one survives as a conscious being, either as one of the saved in the company of God or as one of the damned suffering the eternal torment of separation from God. So, if I want to maintain that the view I am claiming to be the true religion is consistent with true Christianity, I would need to argue that true Christianity doesn't require one to believe that one will literally be revived after death, by God, to enjoy (or suffer) conscious life again.

First, we should note that among those who would insist on a literal interpretation there is a lot of vagueness and confusion about what, exactly, is to be literally believed. I can attest from my own experience teaching introductory philosophy classes that many people who think of themselves as Christians believe in the immortality of the soul separate from the body. They believe that when a person dies, the soul is separated from the disposable body and immediately goes to heaven (or hell or purgatory - but no one believes their loved ones go anywhere but heaven). When asked how a disembodied soul can see or hear or talk to other disembodied souls, they either just assert that a body is not required for that, or they speculate that the soul will have a "spiritual body" of some sort.

Now, this popular view is not the original Christian view, as stated in the historical formulations of Christian dogma.[14] The Apostles' Creed says, in part:

> I believe in the Holy Spirit, the holy catholic church,
> the communion of saints,
> the forgiveness of sins,
> the resurrection of the body,
> and life everlasting.

The Nicene Creed speaks of the Second Coming and Judgment Day:

> He shall come again, with glory, to judge the quick and the dead; whose kingdom shall have no end.

It continues:

> I look for the resurrection of the dead, and the life of the world to come.

The Athanasian Creed contains these words:

> He ascended into heaven, He sitteth on the right hand of the Father, God Almighty;
> From thence He shall come to judge the living and the dead.
> At whose coming all men shall rise again with their bodies;
> And shall give account of their own works.
> And they that have done good shall go into life everlasting, and they that have done evil into everlasting fire.

This is the catholic faith, which except a man believe faithfully, he cannot be saved.

The Augsburg Confession says of Christ's Return to Judgment:

Also they teach that at the Consummation of the World Christ will appear for judgment, and will raise up all the dead; He will give to the godly and elect eternal life and everlasting joys, but ungodly men and devils He will condemn to be tormented without end.

There is nothing in these historical statements of the Christian faith about disembodied souls that rise up to heaven or down to hell immediately upon a person's death, as in the popular version wherein children are told that Grandpa is now up in heaven. Rather, unless Judgment Day comes within our own lifetimes, we will all die and stay dead until Jesus comes back on Judgment Day and raises up our dead bodies. Then and only then will we begin to live again, either in unmixed joy or unmixed torment forever and ever.

Now, one could defend the popular version by saying that upon being raised from the dead, it will be, subjectively, as if no time has passed since the moment of one's death; so that, practically speaking, the dead are already there, enjoying eternal bliss or suffering eternal torment. However, if one wants to insist on a literal interpretation of the original Christian doctrine, then one would have to admit that Grandpa is not up in heaven, enjoying being with Jesus and those who died before him. Rather, he is stone cold unconscious and moldering in the grave (or is a heap of ashes), and, except for Jesus, so are all the other people who have died since the beginning of humanity. When it pleases God at some time in the future, God will reconstitute their bodies and bring them up from the grave, or out of the urn, as if they had never died, as alive as you and I are right now. They and we will then be transformed so as to live on forever, never to die again, and will either enjoy constant pure joy or else will do nothing but suffer horribly with absolutely no relief.

Let's put aside for a moment the question of whether we have good reason to believe that this original Christian doctrine is true, and ask instead whether we want it to be true. That may be hard to do if you already believe this doctrine, or at least believe that you should believe it, even if you're not sure. Likewise, if you already disbelieve this doctrine, you are likely to think that it is irrelevant whether you want to believe it. Facts are facts, and you shouldn't believe something just because you would want it to be true. I'm suggesting, though, that it can be useful as a thought experiment to imagine away what you already believe and what you think you should believe, and ask yourself what you would want to believe about this subject, if you could just believe whatever you wanted and if what you wanted to believe would come true, so that your belief would be not just pleasant but also correct. That way, when you go on to ask whether you have good reason to believe the doctrine in question, it will be easier to detect, and put aside, any influence of the secret heart's desire on your deliberations. Then, if it does fortunately turn out that what you want to be true coincides with what you have good reason to believe *is* true, you will have as much reassurance as you can get that you aren't simply deceiving yourself.

Do you want the following to be true? Unless Jesus comes back before you die, there will inevitably come a day when you will die and stay dead for an undetermined length of time, until Jesus comes and makes you live again, never to die again, but in such a way that your life from then on would not be a mixture of joy and suffering as it is now but instead would be either pure joy or pure suffering, depending on Jesus' judgment of you. And it is not that you are an exception. This is what happens to everybody. For discussion purposes, let's call this "the original Christian doctrine," since that's what it is.

Again, some people think they know already that this is true. Or, they might say that they don't know but they have faith that it is true. Others think they know, already, that it isn't true. Others think they neither know nor have faith. It could be that those in the first group are right, or it could be that those in the second group are right. However, these are mutually exclusive alternatives. On the other hand, those in the third group could also be right, either way. Whether the believers are right or the deniers are, the agnostics could still be right about their own lack of knowledge and faith. Or, it could be that the agnostics, members of the third group, are deceiving themselves and that deep down they really do know (or have faith) that it is true, or that deep down they really do know it isn't true. I propose that to whichever group you belong, it will be a useful way of answering potential critics from the other groups and of strengthening your conviction, to pretend you have no actual opinion, for the moment, on whether the situation as described in the previous paragraph is the way things are. Instead, ask: If I could make it however I wanted, would this be the way I would want my life to go? Or, would I prefer some other arrangement?

Let's consider alternatives. One of them, already mentioned, is the popular belief in an immortal soul that is not dependent on the body and that separates from the body at death, so that one continues to exist and to be conscious and self-aware, as a disembodied soul. Apparently, on this view, whether one gets a new body or not is irrelevant, because one's identity depends only on one's existence as a soul.

This alternative view may be attractive because it evades the question, firmly answered by the original Christian doctrine, of the quality of that continued existence, and provides a vague reassurance that death is not the end. The original Christian doctrine tells us that our continued existence will be unlike our present existence in that it will be either purely delightful or completely horrible. Would we prefer a vague reassurance of our continued existence over the stark alternative of facing either everlasting joy or everlasting suffering? When we put the question this way, it is clear that it all depends on the quality of the continued existence we would have as disembodied (or possibly reincarnated) souls. Is that continued existence also subject to the stark alternatives of either pure joy forever or pure torment forever? If so, then the only differences between our fates according to the independent soul theory and according to the original Christian doctrine are whether or not we will definitely have bodies and whether or not there most likely will be a period of time during which we are simply dead. As far as I can see, these differences don't give us a clear reason to wish for a future existence according to the independent soul theory rather than one according to the original Christian doctrine. What would matter overwhelmingly would be whether we would get everlasting joy or everlasting suffering. It wouldn't matter so much whether or not we had bodies and whether or not there was an interim period during which we were dead and unconscious. It is likely that what makes the independent soul theory attractive is that we're not sure we want to be faced with the stark alternative of pure joy or pure horror, and that the vagueness of the theory (What would it be like to exist without a body?) allows us to avoid it and vaguely surmise that we will be able to go on, somehow, much as we have, with a mixture of joy and sadness and, hopefully, a preponderance of the former.

Another alternative possibility to consider is that on some future day not of our choosing (unless we decide to commit suicide) we will die and stay dead. This arrangement seems to be worse than being resurrected to everlasting joy but better than being resurrected to everlasting suffering. From a selfish point of view, if one has the gift of grace and rests assured that one is among the saved who will have everlasting joy, one would be reluctant to trade this for simple mortality. However, since according to the original Christian doctrine, there are some who are damned to everlasting torment; in the interest of justice, it seems preferable for the fate of everyone to be eventual death with no resurrection. Inflicting pure torture forever and ever would not be a just punishment for even the greatest evil that a human being could do, and Christians admit that no one actually deserves everlasting joy, since it is a gift graciously given by God in spite of our sins.

So far, it simply isn't clear that our ultimate fates as described in the original Christian doctrine are what we would wish for, but as long as we are just thinking about what we would prefer, if we had a choice, it may be helpful to consider some other alternatives.

One such possibility would be that you simply never die in the first place and instead you would go on living pretty much as you have been living, with a mixture of joys and sorrows, in sickness and in health, forever and ever. For comparison, let's stipulate here, and in all the following alternative possibilities, that you are not an exception; that is, that we are describing the general situation for every human being. For a fair comparison with the original Christian doctrine, let's also say that Jesus will take care of the problem of overpopulation, that would result if no one ever dies, in the same way (however that is) that He would take care of it if everyone is brought back from the dead on Judgment Day.

There are two notable differences between this imaginary scenario that we might call "biological immortality" and the situation as described in the original Christian doctrine. 1) In biological immortality, there is no gap over an undetermined length of time between death and resurrection, while there is such a gap in the situation as described in the original Christian doctrine. 2) In biological immortality life goes on as it has already, as a mixture of joy and suffering with, possibly, at most, brief periods of pure joy and of pure suffering; whereas in the situation of the original Christian doctrine, the resurrected life is either pure joy or pure suffering. I can't see that the first of these differences is important, since, as I noted above, there would be no subjective experience of the passage of time during a period of any length while one is completely unconscious. So, as long as life is guaranteed to go on as before, after a temporary loss of consciousness, a life without such a gap wouldn't be better than one with one. The really significant difference between 1) the situation we are calling biological immortality and 2) that as described in the original Christian doctrine is that, in (2) after the gap, life is no longer a mixture of joy and sorrow, sickness and health, but is one everlasting experience of pure joy or pure suffering, whereas in (1) we have just an everlasting continuation of a mixture of joy and sorrow. If you had to choose between the two, and if there were no consideration you had to take into account other than your own preference, which of these two situations would you want to be what happens to people?

Christian salvation-or-damnation seems like a gamble compared to biological immortality. With the latter, you get to keep what you've already been having, forever. With the former, you get either something much better or much worse, forever. Well, some people love to gamble, others don't, and I'm not going to argue either that risk-loving or that risk-aversion is in general better than the other. I simply note, in this connection, that the stakes at risk in Christian salvation-or-damnation are the highest imaginable.

One potential problem with biological immortality that doesn't arise in Christian salvation-or-damnation is the problem of boredom. If one lives forever, wouldn't one eventually get bored with it all? Eventually, wouldn't one have done, over and over again, everything there is to do? This problem might turn out to be naturally solved by memory loss. If you don't remember having experienced something before, then your experience of it again would be subjectively like the very first experience of it. So, we could posit a new, improved version of biological immortality, and stipulate that even though you would live forever, memory loss would ensure that it would never seem to you that you had lived any longer than, say, 150 years. Then, either you wouldn't know that you were actually immortal, or you would know it but you would also know that you would go on to live an unlimited number of disconnected lives and that you have likely already lived a great number of disconnected lives of which you have no memory. The result for biological immortality would be that either one would eventually suffer from intense boredom (in the old version), or else one would live a series of psychologically disconnected lives (in the new version). The first possibility is undesirable, and the second one, though better than the first, doesn't seem to be any better than what we already have, as mortals, supposing we have neither Christian immortality nor a miraculous biological immortality. If there is no psychological connection between my present life and past or future ones, then I might as well be mortal anyway, with a limited number of years to live out what really counts as my life, and believing that there are other people who lived before me, and that, in all likelihood, there will be many more who will live after I am gone.

With Christian salvation-or-damnation, one doesn't get the boredom problem, unless it turns out both that one is damned and that boredom is the worst kind of suffering imaginable. If we are saved, then by stipulation we will never get bored. We will have everlasting joy, and joy is not boring. With boredom factored in, then, we might be inclined to choose Christian salvation-or-damnation over biological immortality. However, there is that enormous, highest-stakes-of-all risk. We might get everlasting joy, but we might also get everlasting unmixed horror.

Let's consider two more alternative possibilities, for comparison, in order to help us decide if we would really want Christian salvation-or-damnation, supposing we had a choice. We could eliminate the undesirable features of biological immortality and of Christian salvation-or-damnation, to get two new choices. Our new choices would be: 1) biological immortality for as long as we want it, and 2) Christian salvation without the risk of damnation. The problem of intense boredom would be eliminated in both. With the first possibility there would be the normal risk of boredom we suffer in our mortal lives, but we wouldn't need to worry about the all-encompassing boredom that would result from eventually having done everything there is to do, over and over again, countless times. We could avoid that simply by choosing to die. This would seem to be an improvement over our mortal lives as we know them, though, in that we wouldn't have to worry about death's coming against our will. With the second possibility, there wouldn't be a risk of boredom or of anything unpleasant.

An interesting thing has happened with our two new choices, when we factor in our risk-loving versus risk-averse propensities. When we were comparing biological immortality-with-no-possibility-of-dying and Christian salvation-or-damnation, our love of risk would have favored Christian salvation-or-damnation, and our aversion to it would have favored biological immortality. Now, however, when we compare biological immortality-for-as-long-as-we-want-it and Christian salvation-with-no-possibility-of-damnation, there is no longer any risk at all in the latter. With biological immortality where we can die if we want but not before we want, we have removed the risk of dying against our will, but there are still all the other risks of ordinary life. We still risk suffering. We are not guaranteed joy.

Then perhaps our only reason not to choose to have guaranteed joy would be that we would be foregoing the thrill of gambling and winning. There is a paradox lurking here, though; for if the thrill of taking a risk forms part of our concept of joy, then it should be included in the pure joy we would be guaranteed to get forever and ever if we were to choose Christian salvation-with-no-possibility-of-damnation. However, the joy of risk-taking can't be included in the everlasting pure joy unless that purity is adulterated with at least the possibility of some

31

undesirable outcomes. Then, depending on which possible undesirable outcomes we include, we would no longer have Christian salvation-with-no-possibility-of-damnation, but instead would have one of the other alternatives we've been considering. We either add back the risk of everlasting pure suffering, and get the alternative of Christian salvation-or-damnation; or, we include the risk of intense boredom, along with the everyday risk of suffering, and get biological immortality; or, we include the everyday risk of suffering without the risk of intense boredom, and get biological immortality-for-as-long-as-we-want-it.

Now, to speak of "gambling," "the thrill of taking a risk and winning," and "the highest stakes imaginable" might seem tawdry, like hoping to win money rather than having to work for it. So, one might be inclined at this point to say, 'I don't need such thrills. So, it doesn't bother me that Christian salvation-with-no-possibility-of-damnation excludes risk. Therefore, it is obviously the best choice.' This would be a mistake, though, because we could pose the same problem in the nobler-sounding terms of the feeling of accomplishment that comes with overcoming adversity, or, more humbly, the simple joy of solving problems. The frustration by the obstacle comes first; otherwise, one doesn't get the joy of overcoming it.

We might still think that Christian salvation-without-the-possibility-of-damnation would be the best choice, on the grounds that its pure, everlasting joy would be the reward for having endured all the problems and frustrations of our lives before death and resurrection. However, since our lives are so short, compared to forever, only a tiny fraction of the pure everlasting joy of salvation could be the kind of joy that comes from solving a problem. The "solution" would be so immeasurably greater than the "problem" as to make it practically non-existent in the first place. So, the result still holds. If we want the kind of joy that comes from the thrill of taking a risk, overcoming adversity, or solving a problem, we should choose one of the other alternatives, and not Christian salvation-with-no-possibility-of-damnation. By the way, similar reasoning shows why it is also unreasonable to think it would be a good thing to include the possibility of damnation after all, on the grounds that it is needed to ensure that evil people are punished. As I noted above, as a reason for rejecting a selfish choice of Christian salvation-or-damnation by someone who has the grace of being assured of being among the saved, no human being could do an evil so great as to deserve pure torture forever and ever.

Before thinking about which alternative among the others is preferable, we should consider doing without the kind of joy that comes from taking risks, overcoming obstacles, solving problems. A former teacher of mine once remarked that the best reason for being happy is no reason at all. Joy, after all, doesn't require any external justification. It is its own justification. So, perhaps there is a kind of joy that doesn't have to be earned by taking a risk or solving a problem, and that is the pure everlasting joy that we would be choosing if we were to choose Christian salvation-without-the-possibility-of-damnation.

The problem, however, is that we have to ponder this question from the point of view of our lives as we know them, since that is the only point of view any of us has. Trying to imagine what this pure everlasting joy would be like, one can call to mind a moment of happiness that just came, with no need of explanation, and then try to imagine that it just stays and never fades away, never goes away and comes back, but just stays. The first part is easy enough, and pleasant, and it would probably do us all good to pause now and then and call such moments to mind. But the second part, imaginatively hanging on to such a moment of happiness, is difficult, because contrary to experience. Such moments go just as they come, and it is very difficult to imagine what one's life would be like if it consisted of an unending happy moment, or an unending series of equally happy moments, each one giving way to the next. That is, it is hard to imagine any details. Imagining it in broad and fuzzy outline is pleasant.

There is a general problem that it is difficult to imagine any kind of life going on forever, and we have that problem just as much in trying to imagine our lives, just as they are, continuing forever (biological immortality), but there is a special problem in imagining what pure everlasting joy would be like. Forgetting about the fact that it is supposed to last forever, it is hard to imagine even what one day of it would be like. What would one do? What would one's emotional state be like? We're saying, of course, that it would be pure joy. It seems to follow that one would never be sad, angry, frustrated, or confused, unless there are joyful ways of experiencing those states of mind. Maybe it would be that there would be problems to solve, but that one would be just as glad at having the problem to solve as one would be when one had solved it. It would have to be, though, that one would also be just as glad if one failed to solve it. We've probably all experienced fleeting carefree moods when life is like that. Would we want life to be like that always? Maybe so. But now when we add back the general problem and remember that we are supposing that our lives will go on forever like this, I am even less sure that this would be desirable. It's quite clear to me that I wouldn't want to go on and on experiencing ecstasy. I think "nearly unbearable ecstasy" would eventually become literally unbearable. But I'm inclined to think that even perfectly smooth, carefree contentment should eventually come to an end. Or, at least, I would want that option.

This gives us a new option to consider: everlasting joy-for-as-long-as-we-want-it. Of the options we have considered, both this new option and biological immortality-for-as-long-as-we-want-it seem preferable over the options of 1) the unalterably permanent salvation-or-damnation of the original Christian doctrine, 2) unalterably permanent salvation-without-the-possibility-of-damnation, and 3) unalterably permanent biological immortality. However, it isn't entirely clear whether everlasting joy-for-as-long-as-we-want-it or biological immortality-for-as-long-as-we-want-it is preferable. In one way, everlasting joy-for-as-long-as-we-want-it is preferable, because it removes all possibility of suffering and instead guarantees pure joy. In another way, biological immortality-for-as-long-as-we-want-it is preferable, because it would be more like the life we already know, and this is easier to imagine in detail, and somehow familiar details are pleasing. Either way, though, we have answered our question about the original Christian doctrine according to which each of us will be resurrected on Judgment Day to then live again either in pure joy or in pure torment, forever and ever. Is this how we would want it to be, if we had a choice? The answer is No. If it were simply a matter of preference, it would be a crazy preference to choose to include the possibility of damnation, and it would be prudent to include an "as long as I want it" opt-out clause even for the choice of everlasting joy, if for no other reason than that it is so difficult to imagine any details of what it would be like for life to be just one unending happy moment, or an unending series of happy moments.

Furthermore, the difficulty of imagining a life of pure, everlasting joy gives us a reason to prefer the only kind of joy we do know: the joy that comes in our mortal lives as we know them. Since death is bad because it takes away the possibility of any more such joys, we might prefer to go on living forever with lives as we know them, a mixture of joys and sorrows, with the escape clause that if those joys eventually pall or if they give way to an unbearable preponderance of suffering, one could kill oneself. However, it isn't clear to me that it would be irrational to prefer simple mortality over this alternative. To the degree that it seems probable that one would eventually get bored with an unending life or else would eventually fall into a period of unbearable suffering and decide to end it all, a mortal life that ends against one's will, because life still seems precious, might well be preferable.

Now, all this might seem to be a silly, academic exercise. After all, we don't get to choose between Christian salvation-or-damnation and the other alternative fates we have been considering. This is one of those things that are outside our control. Either the original Christian doctrine is true or it isn't, and our hoping it is true or hoping that it isn't won't make any difference. I've already given one answer to this objection. Deciding whether we have good reason to believe the original Christian doctrine is at least partially under our control, and being clear about whether or not we hope it is true helps reveal what is really at issue and makes us aware of our biases. In addition, we should note that from the traditional Christian viewpoint, it can't be right that it won't make any difference what we hope. Hope and faith are related in the following way. Someone who has faith no longer needs merely to hope, but no one has faith in what she or he hopes isn't the case. You may believe, and you may know, that something is true even though it is contrary to what you had hoped, but no one would call that kind of belief or knowledge "faith." Now, since it is supposed to be a matter of faith that the original Christian doctrine is true, that we will all be resurrected on Judgment Day and then live on in pure joy or in pure torment forever and ever; it follows that we have already done much to undermine that faith, by deciding that we aren't even sure that we hope that it is true. Our faith, if we are to have it, will be in something else and not in a literal acceptance of the original Christian doctrine.

Still, unless we are content to be self-deceivers, we need to examine the question of whether we have good reason to believe the original Christian doctrine. If we do, then we should accept it, not as a matter of faith, but just because we think it's true, even if we don't want it to be true. If not, then we need to think about what we could have faith in, if anything.

Chapter 4

The God/Universe Problem

How are we to conceive of God?

They heard the sound of the Lord God walking in the garden at the time of the evening breeze, and the man and his wife hid themselves from the presence of the Lord God among the trees of the garden.

Genesis 3.8

In Chapters 1 and 2 I stated what I take to be some fundamental principles of the true religion, which, for lack of a better term, I've called "individualistic religion." Principle One: everything is fundamentally all right; because, Principle Two: if it would be a bad thing for life to be meaningless (and it is), then life is not meaningless; and because, Principle Three: death can't wipe out the objective meaningfulness of subjective experiences that have already happened; and therefore, Principle Four: we should hope that life is just as fresh and astonishing at the end as at the beginning. I also stated, promising to explain later, that I don't identify myself as a Christian, although I expressed a hope that individualistic religion is consistent with true Christianity. In Chapter 3 I began that explanation with an examination of the question of whether the ultimate fate of all of us as described in the original Christian doctrine is what we would hope for. In this chapter let's continue by asking what reasons we have to accept or to reject a literal interpretation of the original Christian doctrine, and then ask what reasons we have to accept or to reject a symbolic interpretation of it.

A reason to believe in a literal interpretation is that it was formulated by men who were inspired by God, and who were following the word of God as revealed in the Bible. If we allow for figurative or symbolic interpretation, then it all becomes just too subjective, and anyone can make it mean whatever she or he wants it to mean. This reasoning alone is unconvincing, though, because the Bible is full of passages that expressly call for figurative or symbolic interpretation, such as the parables of Jesus himself, which are clearly intended to have a definite, if sometimes obscure, meaning.

A logically prior question is how we are to conceive of God. Believing in God is one way, historically the most popular way, of trying to deal with the fact that there are important things over which we have no control. To believe in God is to believe that there is a person, who is not a human being and who is in control of everything that He or She chooses to control. God exercises this control in the same way that we exercise control over the things that we can control: simply by deciding to. Just as I can freely decide what word I'm going to write next, or whether to turn my head this way or that, or anything else that is physically and psychologically possible for me to do; God can freely decide to do anything that is logically possible. God can change the physical laws of nature. God can create or destroy anything at any time. God can make me believe that I am freely deciding what to write next while actually She or He controls it; or God can decide to leave it up to me what to write next. God can control whatever He or She wants to control, but can also decide to let something go out of His or Her control, just as we can do with regard to things that are under our control. We can decide to intervene or we can step back and watch how things develop, knowing that we can step in and take control whenever we want. For God, everything that happens is like that.

To believe in God, then, is to deal with the fact that there are important things not under our control by believing that these things are at least under the control of someone. God is in charge, and if we have the right kind of relationship with God, then even though, in so many cases, we can't control what happens, we can be sure that everything is fundamentally all right. What really matters to us most of all is not the fulfillment of every particular desire that we have, since we find by experience that the frustration of a particular desire sometimes turns out for the best. It follows that if we can realize that God exists and that She or He wants what is best for us, then it won't matter that there are important things we can't control. Everything would be guaranteed, by God, to be fundamentally all right. However, it doesn't follow that if we can't get ourselves to believe that God exists and that He or She wants what is best for us, then everything is not fundamentally all right. It could be that everything is fundamentally all right whether or not God exists. It could even be that everything is fundamentally all right only if God doesn't exist. That might be the case if we find ourselves unable to be sure that God wants what is best for us.

Our next question, then, is whether, and if so, to what degree, belief is voluntary. Is it possible to choose to believe something or to disbelieve it? Or is it instead that we simply find ourselves believing certain things and disbelieving others? To say that believing in God is a way of dealing with the fact that there are important things outside one's control seems to imply that one chooses to believe this as a way of dealing with that, and people sometimes do say, 'I choose to believe that such-and-such.' However, it is in just such cases that one wonders whether or not they really believe it or are just hoping it is true. If we take an ordinary example of a belief, to say that one chooses to believe it actually just calls into question whether or not it is really true. 'I choose to believe there is some salmon left in the freezer that we can have for dinner tonight.' This could be a way of facetiously expressing the hope that there is. In contrast, if you just checked five minutes ago and saw some salmon in the freezer, you wouldn't need to choose to believe it. You would just believe it. So, when I characterize belief in God as a way of dealing with the fact that there are important things outside one's control, I'm not suggesting that this is the explanation for why everyone who believes in God does so, as if to say that they choose to believe in God, in a way that implies they don't really have a good reason and are just hoping. We have yet to determine if that is the case.

There is another locution that paints a more accurate picture of the relation between the will and belief, and that is: 'I've decided that I believe such-and-such.' Contrary to surface appearances, this doesn't imply that you can simply make a decision to believe the thing in question and thereby find yourself believing it. What you can do is to decide to examine your beliefs more closely, to keep an open mind, to take in new information, to consider arguments pro and con, and then you may find that you have a definite belief that you did not have before. You may even find that you have changed your mind, that you don't really believe, after all, what you thought you believed before. That is when you might announce, 'I've decided that I believe such-and-such.' Or, you may find that you are even more convinced of your original belief, so that you would say, 'I've decided that I still believe such-and-such.' It is in this spirit that we should try to find out what we believe about God and the original Christian doctrine.

A few paragraphs back, I sketched what I take to be a non-controversial view of the conception of God's powers relative to ours, namely that God, if He or She exists, is vastly more powerful than we are, but also that God is a person, though not a human being. God's powers are not impersonal forces, like the power of a magnet to attract iron filings or the power of water to dissolve salt. Rather, they are like the powers you or I have to choose to do or not to do something, either for some reason, or on a whim.

Although there is some controversy about whether the God of Judaism and the God of Christianity are one and the same, at least we know that, on both views, He has the very definite personality that is expressed in the Hebrew Bible and the Old Testament. Although sometimes likened to a female, He is usually masculine.

He demands loyalty, is jealous and easily angered, but is also just and merciful; at least so He says, and so He sometimes needs to be reminded. As Jack Miles convincingly shows in *God: A Biography*, God comes to know Himself through creating us in his own image, but at critical points He worries about the experiment getting out of control.[15] He revokes the natural immortality He had originally given to human beings, as punishment for Adam and Eve's disobeying the one simple rule He had imposed upon them: not to eat the fruit of the tree of the knowledge of good and evil. He is frequently disappointed in us. He needs for us to acknowledge Him as God in order to know Himself as God. He is utterly unlike the self-sufficient gods as Epicurus describes them, beings who, knowing no trouble in mind or body, couldn't care less about what we think about them and thus have no motive to reward or to punish us for anything. Of course, that makes Him much more interesting to us. He worries about us, and so we have to worry about Him and what He will do. He is so awesomely powerful that, with few exceptions, it is fatal even to see Him. His very name is to be held in awe. It means 'I am what I am' or 'I will be what I will be,' and indicates His unconditional independence of us; but as Miles argues, this is a boast rather than a reality, since He needs a people to acknowledge Him as God in order to know Himself as God.[16]

Then, on the Christian but not the Jewish view, this very same God at a certain time decides to become a human being, and one who has extraordinary insight and powers, for a human being. He teaches that everything is about to change for the better in a fundamentally important way. He gathers a following, but powerful figures don't believe Him and see Him as a threat. They contrive a sham trial, and then have him tortured and executed. By becoming mortal Himself and enduring humiliation and a painful death, God shows that death can be overcome after all, and that He has changed his mind and gives back to those who believe in Him the eternal life that He had taken away from all human beings when He punished Adam and Eve.

On the third day after His execution, He comes back to life, appears to His disciples, instructs them to carry on the work, and then ascends into Heaven. He will return soon to judge the living and the dead. Then, those who have done good will get everlasting joy. Those who have done evil will get everlasting punishment.

Is this conception of God literally true? If it is, and if we are sure that we understand it and have some way of being sure it is true, then we certainly have a good reason to believe in the original Christian doctrine about our ultimate fates, since the conception contains the doctrine. If it is not literally true, then is it true in a symbolic or figurative or, say, poetic, way? If so, then we wouldn't have a good reason to believe in a literal interpretation of the original Christian doctrine, but we would have a good reason to believe that it symbolizes something true. Or, is this conception of God just false through and through: false both literally and, like bad art, false in the sense of being degrading rather than uplifting to our spirits?

As I mentioned above, one reason against insisting on a literal interpretation is that the Bible contains many passages that obviously are intended symbolically or figuratively rather than literally, because they are so interpreted in the Bible itself. For examples, there are the accounts of Joseph's and Jacob's dreams and Jesus' parables. This reason alone is insufficient, though, because the Bible also contains claims that are just as obviously meant to be accepted as historical fact. We have corroborating independent evidence for some of those claims, in the form of archaeological finds and extra-Biblical historical records. However, for many others we will probably never have any evidence other than the Bible itself. For example, is it really literally true that the Lord God walked in the garden at the time of the evening breeze, making a sound, so that Adam and Eve hid from Him, because they had eaten the forbidden fruit? (Gen. 3.8) Does God literally have a physical body, as He must have had in order to walk in the garden, making a sound; and to talk with Adam and Eve, Moses, Aaron, and Samuel (Ex. and 1 Sam.); and to wrestle with Jacob? (Gen. 32.24-32) Since God can freely decide to do anything that is logically possible, then He can have any kind of body He wants or no body at all. Does He have a body now?

It will do no good to dismiss this as a silly question and at the same time to claim to believe in a literal interpretation of the original Christian doctrine. Either God has a body or He doesn't. "Having a body" includes any kind of physical existence, such as that of a human body or other recognizable physical object large or small, but also that of being the physical universe itself or any part of it, including theoretical physical entities like quasars, quarks, and fields of force. "Not having a body" includes any kind of non-physical existence, such as that of being a Platonic Form; an immaterial mind, soul, spirit, or Neo-Platonic Source of Being; an abstract idea; a number. As He is portrayed in the Bible, God at least sometimes has a body, as in the aforementioned cases of walking in the garden; talking to Moses, Aaron, and Samuel; wrestling with Jacob; and also as a burning bush, as a pillar of cloud and a pillar of fire; and also as the human being, Jesus of Nazareth. In other passages, God is an (immaterial?) Spirit, as when the Spirit of the Lord comes upon Saul (1 Sam. 11.6) and David (1 Sam. 16.13), and when Jesus promises that the Father will send the Holy Spirit after Jesus goes to the Father (John 14.26). In John 1.1, famously, God is the Word that became flesh. The Apostle's Creed states that God is the Creator of heaven and earth.

There are only two possibilities consistent with a literal interpretation of this view. One is that God has always had a body, so that when He created heaven and earth He created only a new part of the physical universe, in addition to the part that must have already been there for Him to inhabit. The other is that God had no body, and there was no physical universe at all until He created it, so that His creation of heaven and earth really means the creation of the entire physical universe. Having created it, He can then become, for as long or short a period as He chooses, any particular part of it or none at all.

If God has always had a body and has one now, then it is a job for physical science to discover what part of the universe is the godly part. Since our current best physical theories make no reference to God, it would have to turn out that the hypothesis that there is such a divine particle or body or force would give us greater predictive power and control than we have now. But even if God did not have a body when He created the universe and does not have one now, if we are to believe literally that He talked to Moses and Aaron, appeared as a pillar of cloud, a pillar of fire, a burning bush, and became Jesus of Nazareth, it is still a job for science to discover how this is possible, since our current best theories make no reference to non-physical entities or forces creating or becoming physical ones.

There is no conceptual problem with the first possibility. It is possible that scientists could yet discover what part of the physical universe is the part that somehow created and sustains all the rest, and that that physical entity could also have the kind of properties that are attributed to a person, with the personality of God as portrayed in the Bible. However, although conceptually possible, there doesn't seem to be any good reason to expect this to happen. In any case, we will just have to wait until it does.

There is a conceptual problem with the second possibility. If God is essentially a supernatural, non-physical being, who nevertheless is able to create physical things and interact with them and even temporarily become them; then we need to understand how it is possible for a non-physical being to have physical effects.

There is an imperfect parallel between this challenge that a literal interpretation forces on our thinking, which we might call "the God/universe problem," and the philosophical problem known as "the mind/body problem." The latter is the problem of understanding how a purely mental, non-physical mind can affect (and be affected by) a purely physical, non-mental body. If we think of God as the mind of the universe, as many Christians do when they argue that the only alternative is to believe that it is just a lucky accident that the fundamental physical constants have the precise values required to make life possible and even luckier that it accidentally evolved into intelligent, complex forms; then the God/universe problem is just the cosmic version of the mind/body problem, with the extra feature that one needs to understand not only how a non-physical God affects an existing physical universe but also how He brought it into existence in the first place. The mind/body problem applies to each of our finite minds and bodies, but there is no corresponding claim that the mind of each person brought that person's body into existence. That is why I said that the parallel between the two philosophical problems is imperfect. But this difference between the two is just as instructive as the similarity, as we shall see.

Historically, the mind/body problem is associated with the name of René Descartes. Descartes argued that reality is made up of two radically different kinds of things: minds and bodies. A mind is a purely mental, unextended (i.e., non-spatial) thing, with no physical properties. A body is an extended (space-occupying) thing, with no mental properties whatsoever. Minds are naturally immortal. Having no spatial parts, they cannot disintegrate the way a physical body can. A person, such as Descartes himself, is essentially a thinking thing, i.e., a mind, since he can conceive of himself existing without a body but not without a mind. It would be a logical contradiction to conceive of himself as a non-thinking thing. (He would be both thinking and non-thinking at the same time.) Minds and mental things and properties in general are the natural province of religion. Bodies and physical things and properties in general are the natural province of science. Thus, science can proceed in its restricted domain free of the dictates of the religious authorities, since it can in no way threaten the truth of religion, which has nothing to do with the merely physical.

Notice that Descartes' demarcation of the boundary between religion and science is quite different from the one that I have been proposing. On my view, some, but not all, physical things and events have religious significance. The difference between science and religion is that science is the kind of understanding that aims to give us predictive power and control, whereas religion is our intellectual and emotional response to things that matter deeply to us that are utterly beyond our control, even with our best science. Descartes' truce between science and religion came at a steep price. He was unable to give an explanation satisfactory to anyone other than himself as to how a person's mind can affect and be affected by his or her body. Similarly, if God is purely non-physical, then how can God affect anything in the physical universe?

The mind/body problem is a problem because the conception of mind and body as radically different kinds of things, that each exists in its own way, conflicts with the belief that mind and body interact in many ways. It just seems obvious that a series of mental events, such as my trying to formulate my thoughts about this topic, results in a series of physical events, such as my fingers moving over a keyboard. And it also seems obvious that a series of physical events, such as light waves impinging on the rods and cones in my eyes, causing changes in the optic nerve, result in a series of mental events, such as my seeing what I've typed and having further thoughts about what to type next.

In order to shed some light on the God/universe problem, let's consider some of the solutions that philosophers have proposed to the mind/body problem. First, there are two diametrically opposed monistic views, each of which simply eliminates one side of the mind/body duality. According to idealism, mind alone exists. Physical objects are just collections of perceptions, with no more mind-independent reality than the things we see in a dream. According to materialism, body alone exists. Thoughts, emotions, and all other mental phenomena are nothing more than biochemical processes in the brain and body. Then there are several varieties of dualistic views. Epiphenomenalism is the view that body and mind both exist, but that they don't causally interact. All causality is physical causality. Mind is like a reflection on water. It is there, but it plays no causal role. Occasionalism is the view that mind and body just appear to interact and that neither of them has any genuine causal efficacy. God actually causes everything to happen both mentally and physically. This view solves the problem of mind/body interaction by moving the entire problem to the problem of God/universe interaction. Descartes' own solution is simply to assert that mind and body interact at the pineal gland. The mind influences and is influenced by the motions of the fluids there, and yet it still somehow remains entirely free of any physical properties.

Some of these solutions have parallels in proposed solutions to the God/universe problem. Again, we have two diametrically opposed monistic views, which solve the problem by simply eliminating one side of the relation. Pantheism is the view that everything is God; i.e., God alone exists. Atheism solves the problem by asserting that the natural universe alone exists. Then we have two dualistic views. They are both rather like Descartes' proposed solution to the mind/body problem, in that they simply assert that there is interaction between God and the universe without explaining how. They differ only in how often this occurs. Deism is the view that God created the universe and imposed a set of natural laws and has had no further interaction with it. Theism is the view that God created the universe and also constantly maintains it, and occasionally intervenes. Theism is the view that is implied in a literal interpretation of the original Christian doctrine.

Notice that the two versions of dualism in regard to the God/universe question are like Descartes' version of dualism, in that they hold there is real causal interaction between God and the universe. There is no God/universe dualism that corresponds to epiphenomenalism. That would be a view that God and the universe are two completely separate realms and that God has no causal influence ever on the universe. As far as I know, no one holds that view. It is somewhat similar to Epicurus' view. As we have seen, he held that the correct conception of the gods is as perfectly blessed, immortal beings who have no interest in human affairs and have no role in creating the universe, which has always existed. However, he seems to have regarded the gods as having natural, physical existence, so his is a monistic view. The gods exist within the physical universe, just like everything else that exists.

None of the classical solutions to the mind/body problem are satisfactory. Idealism and materialism each require us to deny something that seems more obviously true than does either of those theories. Either we must deny that physical objects can exist independently of anyone perceiving them, or we must deny that we actually have conscious experiences.[17] Epiphenomenalism and occasionalism likewise require us to deny what seems more obvious than either of those theories. We must deny that our minds have any effects on our bodies and deny that what happens to our bodies has any effect on our minds. Descartes' own proposed solution is open to the obvious objection that he violates his own thesis about the radically different natures of minds and bodies when he claims that they interact at the pineal gland.

Is there a solution? I think there is, and that philosopher John R. Searle has discovered it. The solution requires rejecting the conception of mind and body as two different kinds of things with no properties in common. Since such a conception implies that mind and body cannot interact, it violates our original conception that, although there is a difference between mental things or events and physical ones, mental things or events can and do affect physical things or events, and vice-versa. Searle argues that we can easily conceive of a clear distinction between the mental and the physical without also making it impossible that the two interact. The problem is that when Descartes elucidated a traditional conception of the difference between the mental and the physical, he included some features for which we can now see there is no good justification and which are the very ones that make it seem impossible for there to be mind/body interaction. The unnecessary and unsupported requirements on the mental side are that the mental must not be spatially located and not extended in space, not explainable by physical processes, and incapable of acting causally on the physical. The unnecessary and unsupported requirements on the physical side are that the physical must be objective, quantitative, and nonintentional, that is, not able to refer to anything beyond itself. As Searle argues,

> There is no reason why a physical system such as a human or animal organism should not have states that are qualitative, subjective, and intentional.

He also argues that there is no reason why a state that is qualitative, subjective, and intentional, i.e., mental, should not have a spatial location, be extended in space, be explainable by physical processes, and be capable of acting causally on the physical.[18]

Similarly, a solution to the God/universe problem requires that we question the assumptions involved in a literal interpretation of the Biblical account of God: specifically, the assumptions that God literally created the universe out of nothing and that He is either a physical entity who interacts with the rest of the physical universe or else a non-physical being who can control any physical event He chooses to control and who can take on physical existence whenever He sees fit. We don't have a clear conception of what it means to say that the universe was created, or that a non-physical being with no physical properties can nevertheless cause physical events. We have a clear conception of how a physical being can cause physical events, but we have no viable scientific hypothesis that identifies any particular physical being as one that has the personality ascribed to God in the Bible and as the one who created all the rest of the physical universe. For these reasons, literal versions of deism and theism fail to solve the God/universe problem. Pantheism would get rid of the problem by simply identifying God with the physical universe, but it is unacceptable because it fails to explain why some things are religiously significant and other things aren't. Atheism also gets rid of the problem, but at the price of failing to explain how anything can be religiously significant.

If we drop the literalist assumptions, we still have something that is religiously significant, namely, the conception of the Biblical account of God as an elaborate symbol for the fact that there are important things beyond our control. What is the relation between this fact and the physical universe? It isn't that this fact is a non-physical entity that somehow created all of physical reality. It is rather that this fact is manifested in various ways in the lives that we live in the physical universe. (I shall argue later that it is also a necessary condition for our lives to be meaningful.) In this way, things or events can have both physical properties and properties of religious significance.

The fear of God and the trust in God form the two-sided personification of the emotions we feel when we confront what is beyond our control. Whether or not something is holy, that is, religiously significant, has nothing to do with whether or not it is physical but only with its significance to us as a sign of the way we are helpless and yet safe.

On this view, the relation between God and the physical world is like the relation between the meanings of words or other symbols and the physical objects - for example ink marks, vibrations in air, pigments on canvas - that are their tokens. What the Bible tells us about God's relation to the physical universe, then, is literally false, but is symbolically true and important as long as we understand it as a symbol of something true and important.

One might think that this is less clear than the thought that God literally created the universe. However, that thought only seems clearer because it is more familiar. If we examine it, we see that it, too, is just a metaphor or a simile, for it is the thought that God's creation of the universe is like a human being's ability to impose order on raw materials, as, for example, when a potter molds clay to make a pot. This was how Plato conceived of the divine demiurge (maker) in the *Timaeus*, that is as an intelligence that imposes order on chaotic material. But we actually understand this comparison less well than we understand the above comparison of the relation between God and the physical world to the relation between the meanings of words or other symbols and their physical tokens. Human beings have physical bodies and couldn't create things without them. If we suppose God has a physical body, then the analogy holds, but we then have the scientific question of where God's body is and what constitutes it. If we suppose God is a non-physical intelligence acting without physical means, then the analogy with humans' creation of objects breaks down. It breaks down even further given the Judeo-Christian idea that God doesn't create things out of pre-existing matter but rather creates matter out of nothing.

It is actually much clearer to compare the relation between God and the physical universe to the relation between the meaning of a word and the marks on a page that symbolize that word. Another comparison would be with the way in which something can be both physical and economically significant. A credit card, for example, is an economically significant thing, and it is also a physical object with purely physical properties. Its properties as an economically significant thing can and do cause changes in the physical world, as when I use it to purchase a tank of gas. Changes in its physical properties can cause changes in its economically significant properties, as when I cut it in two to ensure that neither I nor anyone else uses it again.

Another example is the way in which a thing can have both properties of social significance and physical properties. A wedding ring, for instance, has matrimonial significance (and economic value), as well as purely physical properties.

Am I saying that religion is merely a social construct? No. In the first place, there is nothing "mere" about social significance. In the second place, and more importantly, I would argue that religious significance cannot be created simply by our agreeing to treat certain things as religiously significant, in the way that economic and social significance are created by the conventions of society (although they are no less real for that).

There are two reasons for this. One has to do with the moral component of religious significance, or holiness. It makes sense to think of the economic significance of a currency system and the social significance of a social custom as the results of conventions, with all the objective reality created by the conventions. However, it doesn't make sense to think of morality in the same way. A society could adopt the convention that ritual human sacrifice is moral, but that wouldn't make it moral. There are some things about which one may say, with good reason, 'If you don't recognize that this is immoral, then you simply have no conception of what morality is all about.' I shall say more in a later chapter about the connection between morality and religion. For now, my point is that, because of the moral component of religious significance, we can say, for example, that it is a false belief that ritual human sacrifice is religiously significant in any way that redeems the immorality of it.

The second reason is that the whole point of religion requires that each individual come to understand and appreciate it for himself or herself. This is the principle that was so eloquently defended by John Locke in his justly famous *Letter Concerning Toleration*, as when he wrote that

although the magistrate's opinion in religion be sound, and the way that he appoints be truly evangelical, yet if I be not thoroughly persuaded thereof in my own mind, there will be no safety for me in following it. No way whatsoever that I shall walk in against the dictates of my conscience, will ever bring me to the mansions of the blessed. I may grow rich by an act that I take not delight in; I may be cured of some disease by remedies that I have not faith in; but I cannot be saved by a religion that I distrust, and by a worship that I abhor.[19]

If we understand God as the meaning of the universe, as a symbol for the personal significance, for each of us, of the ways in which we are helpless and yet safe, then we have no God/universe problem. There is no incompatibility between the religious significance that really exists and the physical universe as we know it scientifically. Religion is not a substitute for science, and science is not a substitute for religion.

The original Christian doctrine says that those who have died will be bodily resurrected on Judgment Day and that at that time those who have done good will have everlasting joy and those who have done evil will have everlasting punishment. We previously determined that, at the least, we are not even sure that we hope that this is literally true. Now, we have seen that we have a good reason not to believe that it is, namely that in order for it to be literally true, God would have to be a supernatural entity who created and acts on the physical universe, and this is either a wildly improbable extension of physical science or else it is as unintelligible as mind/body interaction is on the false supposition that minds and bodies have no properties in common. What symbolic meaning, if any, should we give to this doctrine about our ultimate fates? How are we to understand the alternative of everlasting joy or eternal punishment? What, in the reality of our lives corresponds to these ultimately high stakes? Just this: that, although the circumstances of one's death will be one aspect of one's life that could make a difference, the fact that one dies some day and then lives no more forever, has no effect on the character of one's life. It will be eternally true that you had just exactly the life that you did. If your life is worth living and if you do your bit to make the world a better place, it will always be true that that is how your life was. If you make the world worse, it will always be true that your life was a tragic waste. Those are ultimate stakes. It really does matter, as much as anything can matter, which is a lot: just as the original Christian doctrine implies. This is true Christianity, in my humble opinion, but since I am quite aware that the weight of tradition will cause many people who think of themselves as Christians to insist on the literal existence of a supernatural God, I'm quite content to call it just "individualistic religion."

Chapter 5

The Problems of Evil and Suffering

How can it be fundamentally all right that there is evil and suffering?

Sufficient unto the day is the evil thereof.

Matthew 6.34

How can it be fundamentally all right that there are some people who make the world worse and thus have lives that are tragic wastes? This is the problem of evil. How can it be fundamentally all right that we suffer, see our loved ones suffer, and lose them to death? This is the problem of suffering. These two problems are closely related in that the way in which people make the world worse is by causing people or non-human animals to suffer when this easily could and should have been avoided. All of us at times, when we are overcome by emotions such as fear and anger or when we become callously indifferent because we are tired or frustrated, do things that hurt people or animals and thus make the world worse. Our lives would be better if we didn't do that, but they can still be fundamentally all right as long as there are more ways in which we make the world better. That requires that we admit that we have done wrong, because otherwise we won't be motivated to try to make up for it. Notice that I didn't say 'hurt *other* people.' Hurting people includes hurting oneself.

Among the things that death can keep from happening is our admitting a wrong we have done and our trying to make up for it. So, it is possible for a person's net effect on the moral universe to be that he or she made the world worse, and thus it is possible for a person's life to be a tragic waste. So, we are stuck with the problem of explaining how it can be fundamentally all right that

55

some people have lives that are tragic wastes.

Since the evil that such people do is to cause people or animals to suffer for no good reason, it follows that if we can explain how it can be fundamentally all right that people or animals suffer for no good reason, then we would have also have explained how it can be fundamentally all right that some people cause themselves or others to suffer for no good reason. But this sounds very dangerous. Wouldn't we then be justifying the doing of evil acts? Here we see exactly why false religion is so dangerous. If we get the wrong answer to this question, we might become nihilistic torturers and murderers. One wrong answer is to believe in a god who is a nihilistic torturer and murderer himself. Another is to believe that there is no god and that this implies that everything is permitted.

We need to be clear about what we are asking. How can it be all right for someone to suffer for no good reason? That sounds like it is asking how we can justify what can't be justified. Simply as a matter of logic, that is patently impossible. The point of adding the qualifying phrase 'for no good reason' is that if we think there is a good reason why someone is suffering, as for example, when a child is being mildly punished to teach him or her correct behavior or getting an injection to prevent a disease, then there is no problem of explaining how that suffering is justified. We've already explained it. The problem is to explain how it can be all right that children and adults get sick or hurt, whether as victims of disease, accident, animal attack, self-inflicted harm, or crime, when we can't see that it does the victim any good or that she or he in any way deserved it.

The problem of evil, understood as including the problem of suffering, is typically presented as a challenge to theism. If there is an omniscient, omnipotent, and benevolent God, then there would be no evil and people wouldn't suffer. However, there is evil and people do suffer. Therefore, there is no God. The most popular theistic strategy is the free-will defense. The only way that God could guarantee no evil would be to take away our free will and compel us, like puppets or robots, always to do the right thing. However, a world like that wouldn't really be as good as one in which there are moral agents with free will; because, even though free will makes it possible for us to do evil, it also makes it possible for us freely to choose to do good; and this is so valuable as to outweigh the evil that is risked in the process. That may be a convincing theistic answer to the part of our question that asked how it can be all right for us to suffer as the victims of self-inflicted harm or crime, but it is no answer to the part that asks how it can be all right for us to suffer, through no fault of our own, as the victims of illness, accidental injury, or animal attack.

A possible theistic answer to that part of the question is to try to show that it is logically impossible for God to create a world with no suffering that results from illness, accidental injury, or animal attack. Thus, St. Augustine argued that in creating the world, God did not create simply more of Himself, that is, a perfect being. Everything that He creates is good; otherwise, He wouldn't have created it. However, since the things He creates are not themselves the perfect being, they are subject to corruption, and that is what evil is. The corruption of an existing thing is either partial or total. If it is partial, then the thing continues to exist, and that much good remains. But even if the corruption is total, as when someone dies of an illness, the worst that can happen is that the corruption destroys the thing but in the process also destroys itself. Therefore, good is conceptually guaranteed to outweigh evil, and it is fundamentally all right that we suffer from illness, accidental injury, or animal attack, because the only way God could have prevented it would have been not to create us in the first place.[20]

It isn't very important that Augustine's conception of evil, in this argument, is broader than the one we have been considering, i.e., the willful imposition of suffering for no good reason, since the former includes the latter. He may be right that even the rusting of a piece of iron is evil, while even a rusty piece of iron is good. What is important is that if we take the theism in this argument literally, then we have the intractable God/universe problem we discussed in the previous chapter. On the other hand, if we understand God as the symbol of what is beyond our human control, then I don't think I can improve on this line of reasoning as an explanation for why everything is fundamentally all right, even though people suffer.

It is interesting that Epicurus, who didn't believe in a creator God, used similar reasoning to quell anxiety about suffering, arguing that we can take comfort in the fact that there is a natural limit to suffering. We can endure chronic pains because experience teaches us that they are outweighed by the joys of life, and acute pains are transitory. Either we get over them and continue to live lives that are worth living, or we die and are released from all pain.

We can take comfort in the free-will defense and in Augustine's and Epicurus' arguments that show the limits of suffering. As I said in the first chapter, when I claim that everything is fundamentally all right, I'm not claiming that everything is perfect. I don't like to suffer, and I don't like to see anyone suffer, especially people I love. I would prefer a world with less suffering, and I'll do whatever I can to get it. Having limited powers, not being a world creator, I'll take this world that has been given to me. It is fundamentally all right with me.

In addition to the God/universe problem, there is an objection to the literal theistic version of St. Augustine's argument that doesn't apply to the symbolic interpretation; and this gives us another reason to prefer the symbolic interpretation. The objection is that all St. Augustine's argument accomplishes is to explain in general why good is guaranteed to outweigh evil. It doesn't explain why some relatively innocent sufferers have it so much worse than others. Why are some people born with crippling diseases while others thrive throughout a long life with few health problems and then die in their sleep? It isn't fair. Similarly, the free-will defense can explain that since it is better that we have free will than that we be automatons, there can be no guarantee that we won't do evil things; but it can't explain the unfairness by which some people become the victims of someone else's evil act, while other people sail through life relatively unharmed. The advantage that the symbolic interpretation of theism has over the literal interpretation is that, on the symbolic interpretation, we can admit that it isn't fair. The unfairness falls under the "fear of God" side of the personalization of the fact that there are important things outside our control. One can say, in good conscience, 'It is unfair, and that's bad, and I would change it if I could: but still, I'll take this world I've been given.' In contrast, if you literally believe in an all-powerful, all-good God, then you are forced to believe that it is just an illusion that it is unfair, since there must be some way in which God makes it all right. Of course, you will have no way of understanding how God does it, and the morally repugnant temptation will be to believe that those who suffer inordinately somehow deserve to do so. If that temptation is resisted, there is another one waiting, which is the self-defeating notion that being the victim of unfairness in the present somehow guarantees compensation in the future. This is a distortion of the lesson learned through experience that sometimes one should voluntarily undergo suffering in the present in order to avoid worse suffering, or to gain some good, in the future. It is self-defeating because it just leads to more suffering. If you are content to glory in your suffering in your present life rather than in your joys, there is little reason to think you will be any different in the future. I'm not talking about the noble act of facing unavoidable suffering with dignity, but rather of a kind of false thinking that leads to exaggerated self-pity.

As I said above, the problem of evil, understood as including the problem of suffering, is typically presented as a problem for literal theism, but it is also a problem for every philosophy of life, whether religious or non-religious. Someone who thinks that religion is something we would all be better off without, and that the only intelligent way to deal with the fact that there are important things outside our control is to pursue scientific knowledge, doesn't need to worry about explaining why an omniscient, omnipotent, and benevolent God allows evil; but such a person cannot escape the problem of explaining why we can trust that the pursuit of scientific knowledge will result in more good overall than evil. Scientific knowledge makes possible improvements in life-saving and life-enhancing techniques; but, as many have observed, it also makes possible improvements in weapons and torture devices. Even life-saving and life-enhancing techniques sometimes have unintended consequences that turn out to be destructive. Without an explanation of why we can trust that science will lead to more good than evil, a philosophy that sees the pursuit of scientific knowledge as our highest duty will be demoralizing, as when Richard Dawkins writes,

> The universe that we observe has precisely the properties we should expect if there is, at bottom, no design, no purpose, no evil and no good, nothing but blind, pitiless indifference.[21]

In that context, Dawkins was opposing the alternative that there is a benevolent Intelligent Designer who has created the universe. He is right in that we simply have no viable theory as to what part of the physical universe constitutes such a Designer or, if He is non-physical, as to how a non-physical entity or force can have any physical effect. It is a false dichotomy, however, to claim that the only alternative is a universe of blind, pitiless indifference. Just look around and ask yourself if you observe any design, any purpose, any evil, any good, any caring. Ah, but Dawkins said there are none of these properties "at bottom." He must be talking about quarks, electromagnetic fields, genes, and such like. But why look there?

One thing that Dawkins and a literal theist would agree on is that the choice is between a creator God and blind indifference. They just disagree about which alternative is the right one. Literal theists argue that the intelligence of human beings must be the product of a greater intelligence. The alternative, they think, is that everything is just a big accident and ultimately meaningless. But why does it have to be that there must first have been God, the cosmic intelligence, and then the creation of everything else, from the Big Bang[22], if that is the correct cosmological theory, to the evolution of the stars, the origins of life, and eventually of humans, especially given that the continued evolution of the universe will eventually make life impossible once again? Here is an alternative religious view: The evolution of the physical universe led to the existence of intelligent beings, each of whom has ultimate value. The "firstness" of intelligence, meaning, and value, the "beginningness" of 'In the beginning . . .,' is not literally a priority in time, but rather a priority in value. The most important thing doesn't necessarily come at the temporal beginning, or at the end. It might very well come in the middle, and in fact, it does.

When I am grateful for intelligence, meaning, and value, to whom am I grateful? Why not say: to my parents and their parents and all my ancestors and everybody else who has contributed to civilization? Also, to my children and grandchildren and all those who are still contributing to civilization and who will in the future keep it going. I am grateful for everything good. I am grateful to everyone good, and especially to those who have done good things for me personally.

When I am afraid, what am I afraid of? I'm afraid of suffering, of dying, of going crazy, of being unloved and unlovable. Salvation is a combination of the opposite emotion plus the conviction that it is justified. One can't directly produce that emotion, but maybe it is possible to contribute to it indirectly by working on the intellectual conviction that it is justified.

As to suffering, the suffering that I fear is the intensification of some pain that I presently feel or that I remember having felt. The fear is rational to the degree that it motivates me to avoid anything I have good reason to believe likely to produce the pain and instead to do whatever is likely to relieve it. The fear of suffering is irrational, unproductive, and, in a deep sense, false, when it continues despite the fact that I have done everything that I can to avoid and to relieve the pain. It then becomes just a self-inflicted pain in its own right.

As to dying, the only insight I have to offer is the one I've already stated. We have good reasons to believe that death is the end of one's subjective awareness, forever and ever, namely all the evidence that beings with living bodies and functioning brains are the only kind of thing that ever show signs of subjective awareness, and that every one of us who presently is subjectively aware has a living body and a functioning brain. Subjective awareness is an ineliminable part of reality, but it is not all of reality. There are also objective facts that are independent of any one person's subjective awareness. If this were not true, communication would be impossible. Since no one can directly experience anyone else's subjective awareness, what we communicate, when we succeed in communicating, is information that is independent of any one person's subjective awareness, for if it were dependent on someone's subjective awareness, then only that person could be aware of it. Among the objective facts are the facts that each person has exactly the subjective experience that he or she has, and the fact that when a person dies, he or she has no more experience. If this were a lifeless universe, with no intelligent, self-aware creatures who have subjective experiences, then it would be meaningless and valueless. However, the fact that in the past there was a time when there were no intelligent, self-aware individuals, and that in the future there will be again such a time, does not make this a meaningless, valueless universe, since it does include the present time when there are intelligent, self-aware individuals, for whom there is meaning and value. Similarly for each individual, the fact that one's lifespan is finite, and that there will come a time when one no longer has any subjective experiences, does not and will never change the timeless, objective fact that one has just the life that one has.

As for the fear of going crazy, this is the fear of losing control of one's own thoughts and emotions, or of not being able to distinguish between one's own thoughts and emotions and those of someone else. What can help is the reflection that there is something fishy about the idea of controlling one's thoughts and emotions in the first place. When I have a thought, did I decide to have that thought? If so, was that decision based upon deliberation or was it just a whim? If it was just a whim, then there isn't really much difference between deciding to have the thought and just having it. If it was based on deliberation, if I weighed the pros and cons and then decided, on balance, that I had a good reason to think that thought, then we will have the same question about each of those thoughts that constituted the deliberation. Did I first deliberate about whether or not to think them? It is pretty clear that thinking is not so deliberate as all that. Thankfully, there is a lot of free play in our thinking, and thoughts just seem to arise, often prompted by previous thoughts but also often taking unpredictable turns. So, the worry about not being in control over one's own thoughts is really a worry about having unpleasant thoughts. Now, it is desirable to face some unpleasant thoughts. One doesn't want to live in a fool's paradise. The unpleasant thoughts one wants to avoid are ones that are false. Then it helps to recognize that they are false. Obsessive thoughts are ones that are false, but that one doesn't acknowledge to be false. One fears that they may be true. Well, if they are true, then one shouldn't want to quit thinking them until one has done something about them. But if they are false, then the key is to recognize that they are false, and replace them with true thoughts about the same subject. This is a matter of cultivating a good habit to replace a bad one.

In the case of emotions, it is clear from the start that one can't just decide to feel an emotion and thereby feel it, but the emotions we feel are connected with the thoughts that we think and the things that we do, and we have some degree of control over our thoughts and actions. One could even say that as a matter of definition, in order for an action to be an action it has to be under the control of the agent; otherwise, it is a passion, that is, the result of being moved by a force outside one's control. One can choose what to read, what to write, what to say, with whom to associate and so on, and pay attention to the emotional results. Just as the fear of losing control over one's thoughts turns out to be the fear of having unpleasant thoughts that are false, so the fear of losing control over one's emotions turns out to be the fear of feeling unpleasant emotions that are irrational. Being uncontrollably angry, having a panic reaction, feeling irrational guilt: these are the kinds of emotional reactions that can cause one to fear for one's sanity. As with the fear of uncontrollable thoughts, the cure will be to acknowledge that such emotions don't correspond to the reality of one's situation and to cultivate better habits to make this more continually obvious.

As for the fear of being unloved and unlovable, the Christian solution - and one of the features of Christianity that accounts for its success - is that Jesus loves me. This symbolizes the fact that it is simply false that I am unlovable. Believing that one is unlovable is one of the worst things that a person can believe. It destroys the compassion that is the source of morality and leads to obnoxious behavior that causes other people to react in ways that reinforce the belief that one is unlovable. One can make oneself relatively unlovable in this way, but the very fact that one reacts this way to the fear of being unlovable proves that, deep down, one really believes that one deserves to be loved unconditionally.

Deserving unconditional love and actually getting it are two different things. Demanding to be loved unconditionally is not the way to get it. One needs to ask oneself to how many people one is willing to extend one's unconditional love and if one's behavior backs up the answer. You can't love someone without accepting his or her limitations, and let's face it: we are quite limited in the amount of unconditional love we have to distribute. The nice thing is that becoming less demanding of the unconditional love of others makes you more lovable.

These reflections about the problem of evil and these bits of self-help advice are really just reminders that we all need from time to time, some of us more than others and at some times more than others. The point is to become convinced that one is justified in feeling, when it comes, the ecstasy turning into serene contentment that is the opposite of the fear of suffering, of dying, of going crazy, of being unloved and unlovable. The conviction comes automatically then, but in the meantime we have to work at it. This is what is symbolized in Christianity as being tested by God. The ecstasy turning into serene contentment is symbolized as the Kingdom of God.

Chapter 6

Morality and Meaning

Is it true that without God there would be no morality and no meaning?

Socrates: Tell me then, please, to what goal's achievement would service to the gods be contributing?

Plato, in *Euthyphro*, 13e

Without God, there would be no morality and no meaning. Is that true? It is, if we understand God as the symbol for the fact that there are important things that are beyond one's control, but not if we understand God according to a literal interpretation of how He is represented in the Bible.

It is easy to see that if nothing were under my control, then my actions would be neither moral nor immoral. We don't praise or blame someone for something that is completely beyond his or her control. Properly speaking, if nothing were under my control, then there would be no such thing as an action of mine. Even movements of my body, in such a case, would be things that happen to me rather than things that I do. I wouldn't even exist as an agent. I couldn't even wish that things were different, or, instead, decide to accept my fate, since that would require a control over my attitude, and we are supposing I have control over nothing. Clearly, such an existence would be not only one in which I had ceased to be a moral agent, but also one in which I had ceased to have a meaningful human existence.

If we consider the opposite extreme, where everything would be under my control, then the only moral question and the only question that could give any meaning to such an existence would be whether or not I would choose to relinquish some of that control, so that some other agent could exist. Other than that, with no possible frustration of my desires and with no other agents whose interests I could aid or harm, my existence would be just as amoral and meaningless as the one in which I had control over nothing.

It follows that if there is to be morality and meaning in my life, it must be the case that I am in control of some things but that there are also important things beyond my control. Is there another necessary condition for morality and meaning, namely, the existence of an all-powerful god who is either an unidentified part of the physical universe or else a non-physical being who can create and annihilate physical things, change the laws of nature, and become a physical being at will? Some people think the existence of God in this sense is necessary to account for the objectivity of morality and for the meaningfulness of our lives.[23] There is a flaw in this thinking, however, which Plato recognized and expressed in the dialogue *Euthyphro*. If the authority of morality derives from God, is God Himself bound by it? Surely, we want to answer Yes, since God is merciful and just, and an immoral god would not be the true God. However, if morality has no reality independently of God's creation of it, if it depends entirely on His will in creating it, then He could change it any time He pleases, just as He can change the physical laws, either momentarily or permanently. This in turn implies that God is not necessarily merciful and just, since He could have made it immoral to be merciful and just and still could do so at any time He wishes. In fact, if this view of God's powers in relation to morality is correct, there is nothing that we think we know is morally wrong that God could not demand of us by decreeing it the moral thing to do. He could decree that it is moral to torture babies, and it would be so. It will do no good to protest that God simply wouldn't do that, because He is good; since on this view His will alone is what makes something good. The only solution is to reject this view as morally repugnant. God is not a tyrant who creates morality arbitrarily by fiat. Something isn't morally good or morally evil just because God says so. Rather, He says so because it is so. This implies that morality is conceptually independent of a literal creator God. That is the only way in which it makes sense to praise God as a good, merciful, and just God.

The whole point of thinking of God as the creator of morality was to explain why morality is not just subjective and arbitrary; and yet if we accept the literalist view, then it is subjective and arbitrary. Do we agree that morality is not just subjective and arbitrary? We should. If one reflects for a moment on one's thinking, on any occasion in which one complained that something was unfair, it becomes obvious that one would not be willing to accept, as a defense of that action, the reply, 'You're wrong that it was unfair because from my subjective point of view, it was fair, and morality is just whatever I say it is.' The thought was that if we could agree that morality isn't determined by what I say it is or by what you say it is, but only by what God says it is, then we would have an objective way of settling moral controversies. Since we have seen a flaw in this thinking, namely that God is morally praiseworthy only if He does not create morality by fiat, then we either have to come up with some other way of explaining the objectivity of morality; or give up and admit that we don't understand it, although we still believe it is objective; or conclude that it is purely subjective and so everything is permitted.

It will do no good to suppose that society, or any other kind of individual or collective authority, determines morality, because the same argument applies against this new supposed authority that applies against taking God to determine morality by fiat. Either society (or - insert the name of any other proposed authority) simply declares something to be morally acceptable (or unacceptable) and thereby makes it so, or else society recognizes that some things are morally good and others morally bad and declares them to be so because they are. On the first alternative, society is morally good only by definition and not in any independently meaningful sense. Society could even declare that practices that lead to its own destruction are morally good, and on the theory that society is the moral authority, those practices would be good. On the second alternative, society makes its judgments by recognizing some universal standard of morality, and if it does so correctly, we have good reason to follow its advice; but in order to know whether society's standards really are morally correct, we need to understand what makes something moral, or immoral.

Well, then, what does make something moral, or immoral? Moral actions are those that give us all a good reason to have less anxiety about meaninglessness, and less fear of suffering, of dying, of going crazy, of being unloved and unlovable; while immoral actions are those that have the effect of increasing that anxiety or those fears. There is, then, an intimate connection between the true religion and morality. Moral actions are the ones that make salvation, i.e., the realization that everything is fundamentally all right, more likely; while immoral actions are the ones that make it less likely. But it isn't that the true religion creates morality, in the false way it is sometimes supposed that God creates morality; for if that were true, then the true religion could have made it so that actions that make salvation less likely would be the moral ones. Any religion that promotes a morality that leads to more anxiety about meaninglessness, or more fear of suffering, of dying, of going crazy, of being unloved and unlovable, is a false religion. So, religion is just as dependent on morality as morality is on religion. This doesn't imply that people who profess some other religious views or none at all are incapable of acting morally. Rather, it implies that when they do, they are practicing the true religion just as much as anyone ever does.

"Us all" includes everyone assessing the morality of the situation. I hope it is clear that an action taken by someone can give us all a good reason to have less anxiety and fear. Suppose a calm and brave person talks a crazed gunman into laying down his weapon, for example. Or suppose in a desperate situation someone organizes a plan to ration the last remaining food. The actions of the crazed gunman, in contrast, would be an equally obvious example that an action someone takes can give us all a good reason to have more anxiety and fear. A less dramatic example of immorality is the way in which someone's having scrawled illegible graffiti over a street sign gives us all a reason to feel slightly more anxious about meaninglessness.

Many actions, though, will be neither moral nor immoral according to this standard. Such actions are morally permissible. Furthermore, it isn't that we need constantly to be assessing the morality of every action we take. The question only arises when we sense that an action promises to provide a reason for us all to have less anxiety and fear, or when it threatens to provide a reason for us all to have more anxiety and fear. Even then, though, it is sometimes difficult to know which it is, and that is why we continue to have moral controversies.

Take the controversy over the moral permissibility of abortion for example. Suppose a woman who has found out she is pregnant and who has a reason for not wanting to be pregnant is deliberating the moral permissibility of having an abortion. I'm suggesting that the right question for her to ask herself is whether - given all the particulars of her situation, including her expectations about the life of the baby she will likely have if she doesn't have the abortion - having the abortion will give us all a good reason to have less anxiety about meaninglessness, and less fear of suffering, of dying, of going crazy, of being unloved and unlovable; or whether, instead, not having the abortion would give us such a reason. If the former, it would be morally praiseworthy for her to have the abortion. If the latter, it would be morally wrong. If it would do neither, then it is morally permissible. I shall say more, in a later chapter, on the question of when the life of an individual human being comes into existence, and on how a well-reasoned answer to that question is necessary in order to answer the one about the moral permissibility of abortion.

The question as to whether it would be moral for there to be a law prohibiting abortions is a separate, though related, question. Would such a law give us all a good reason to have less of that anxiety and less of those fears, or would it do the reverse? Another example would be the question of whether it is moral to go to war in a particular situation. Would going to war in these circumstances give us all, including the potential enemies, good reason to have less anxiety about meaninglessness, and less fear of suffering, of dying, of going crazy, of being unloved and unlovable; or, would refusing to go to war in these circumstances give us all, enemies and our side, good reason to have less of such anxiety and less of such fears? (It is, of course, important to keep in mind that the circumstances include our estimation of the probable actions of the potential enemy, which are not under our control.)

These examples are not intended to show how this proposed answer to the question of what makes an action moral, or immoral, will dissolve moral controversies. All I'm saying is that these are the right questions to ask when assessing the morality of a particular course of action. There will continue to be disagreements about what the facts are and which circumstances are relevant. The point is that, even with an objective moral standard, moral controversies will continue to exist; and it is unreasonable to expect religion to make them go away.

Someone might object that the answer to the question of what would give us all a good reason to be less anxious and less fearful (or the reverse) is subjective, and so this principle doesn't really give us an objective standard. This objection is based on the fact that feelings of anxiety and fear are subjective feelings that vary from individual to individual. The answer to the objection is that we can and do make distinctions between rational and irrational fears and anxieties, and that this is consistent with taking account of subjective differences. The objective standard appeals to what would give us all a good reason to have less fear and anxiety. This is not to say that just any action that makes anyone feel less fear and anxiety is a moral act and that any action that causes anyone to feel more fearful and anxious is immoral. Giving someone a tranquilizer is not necessarily a moral act, and apprehending a criminal is not necessarily immoral.

Suppose a defendant, who is actually guilty, is waiting to hear the jury's verdict, and so are the relatives of the victim. These two parties are likely to have very different subjective assessments on the question of which verdict will constitute a good reason to feel less anxious and fearful. However, the fact that people disagree is irrelevant to the truth of the moral principle. The principle can't legislate away the fact that people sometimes make false judgments about morality. If we suppose that the defendant really is guilty and knows it, and that the justice system is fair and doesn't deal out unjustly harsh penalties, then a "guilty" verdict will give us all, including the defendant, a good reason to feel less anxious about meaninglessness and less fearful of suffering, of dying, of going crazy, of being unloved and unlovable, than would a "not guilty" verdict. The defendant may not appreciate that fact, but it's possible that he or she will come to understand it eventually. On the assumption that the defendant does not know that he or she is guilty, because he or she is a self-deceiver and has managed to acquire the belief that he or she is innocent, it is even clearer that a guilty verdict is still the best thing for him or her; because self-deception is the royal road to anxiety about meaning-lessness.

In the previous chapter, I addressed the question of how it can be fundamentally all right that some people have lives that are tragic wastes, by combining a free-will defense with an Augustinian/Epicurean explanation of the limits of evil/suffering and with an acceptance of the world in spite of its unfairness (which is not the same as complacently accepting the unfairness). Someone has a life that is a tragic waste if she or he has made the world worse and is prevented by death from admitting it and trying to make up for it. But is simply trying to make up for it good enough? Some people do things so horrible that it seems that nothing they could do after that could possibly make up for it. This conflicts with the Christian idea that no one is beyond redemption. Is that Christian idea wrong, or is there some way in which someone who has done some horribly evil acts can be redeemed? It isn't that such a person can do something that will make it as if he or she had never done those evil things. But this is just a particular case of the general truth that no one can go back and change the past. No one who has done anything morally wrong, no matter how minor, can make it as if she or he never did it. What we can do is to repent sincerely. Any time anyone does that, he or she gives us all a good reason to feel less anxiety about meaninglessness and less fear of suffering, of dying, of going crazy, of being unloved and unlovable. In that way, even someone who has done horribly evil things is not beyond redemption.

The intimate connection between morality and religion, then, is two-fold. First, as we reasoned above, a necessary condition for morality and meaningfulness in one's life is that one be in control of some things but not of everything; and the essence of religion is an individual confronting the fact that there are important things outside his or her control. Secondly, there are two things that mutually depend on each other: 1) a meaningful distinction between morality and immorality and 2) the assurance of the true religion that everything is fundamentally all right. If everything were not fundamentally all right, either because death wipes out the objective meaningfulness of our lives, or because, even if we didn't die, our lives would be meaningless anyway; then there would be no reason to care about being a moral person. If there is no meaningful distinction between morality and immorality, if everything is equally moral or equally immoral, then one would have a good reason to be anxious that life itself is meaningless.

Once again we see the importance of facing anxiety about meaninglessness and of allaying it. In Chapter 2, I argued, following Paul Tillich, that anxiety about meaninglessness presupposes the meaningfulness of the question of whether life is meaningful. The experience of anxiety about meaninglessness shows that life is deeply meaningful, since the very question of its meaningfulness hangs in the balance. In short, since it would be a bad thing for life to be meaningless, then it isn't. I also pointed out that this is not a purely intellectual exercise, and that the happiness and heartbreak we experience in our lives constitute emotional evidence that life is not meaningless. Then, at the beginning of Chapter 3, I promised to say more about tuning in to the meaningfulness of life. The time has come to keep that promise.

By "tuning in to the meaningfulness of life," I mean paying attention to meaningful coincidences. C. G. Jung coined the term "synchronicity" as the name for the principle in nature that is manifested in meaningful coincidences.[24] Is there such a thing as a meaningless coincidence? Those inclined towards scientism would probably say that the question should be: is there such a thing as a meaningful coincidence? Thinking about a couple of Jung's examples will show that no coincidence is absolutely meaningless but that some are relatively meaningless, compared to others.

Of the first sort of example, Jung writes:

When for instance I am faced with the fact that my tram ticket bears the same number as the theater ticket which I buy immediately afterwards, and I receive that same evening a telephone call during which the same number is mentioned again as a telephone number, then a causal connection between these events seems to me improbable in the extreme, although it is obvious that each must have its own causality. I know, on the other hand, that chance happenings have a tendency to fall into aperiodic groupings - necessarily so, because otherwise there would be only a periodic or regular arrangements of events which would by definition exclude chance.[25]

We find it relatively easy to dismiss this sort of example as a meaningless coincidence because of the considerations that Jung mentioned. Consider the example of a mechanism that is designed to produce chance results within certain parameters: a slot machine. If a slot machine always paid off or if it never paid off, then obviously we would be justified in suspecting there was something wrong with its randomizing mechanism. But even if it failed to pay off usually and paid off occasionally, in the way any self-respecting slot machine is supposed to act, there would still be something wrong with it if its pay-off occasions came only at regular intervals, rather than bunching up sometimes between extra-long dry spells. So, hitting a lucky streak in which pay-offs are bunched up is perfectly explainable as mere chance, and does not require some causal explanation (The machine is rigged - in the customer's favor!) or some pseudo-causal, magical explanation (My system works!).

Despite these considerations, however, the coincidence of the repeated number on the tram ticket, the theater ticket, and as the phone number, although merely due to chance - and not a cause and effect relation nor to someone's having selected those three numbered items to bear exactly the same sequence of numbers - is not an absolutely meaningless coincidence. This is because there was an extra requirement in order for these events to constitute a coincidence, namely, that Jung noticed this remarkable repetition of the same number, and not in the interest of financial or any other kind of gain, as in the gambling example, but simply because it seemed to be evidence of some kind of inner connection between events that were not related to each other as cause and effect. "Coincidence" can't mean simply "occurring nearby in time or space." If it did, then for every incident, there would be a coinciding one. Coincidences are the ones we find remarkable, and hence significant, to at least some degree.

That it is a matter of degree is shown by comparing the tram ticket/theater ticket/phone number coincidence to another of Jung's examples. He was treating a young woman who, as he says, 'in spite of efforts made on both sides, proved to be psychologically inaccessible.' He continues:

The difficulty lay in the fact that she always knew better about everything. Her excellent education had provided her with a weapon ideally suited to this purpose, namely a highly polished Cartesian rationalism with an impeccably 'geometrical' idea of reality. After several fruitless attempts to sweeten her rationalism with a somewhat more human understanding, I had to confine myself to the hope that something unexpected and irrational would turn up, something that would burst the intellectual retort into which she had sealed herself. Well, I was sitting opposite her one day, with my back to the window, listening to her flow of rhetoric. She had had an impressive dream the night before, in which someone had given her a golden scarab—a costly piece of jewelry. While she was still telling me this dream, I heard something behind me gently tapping on the window. I turned round and saw that it was a fairly large flying insect that was knocking against the window-pane from outside in an obvious effort to get into the dark room. This seemed to me very strange. I opened the window immediately and caught the insect in the air as it flew in. It was a scarabaeid beetle, or common rose-chafer (*Cetonia aurata*), whose gold-green color most nearly resembles that of a golden scarab. I handed the beetle to my patient with the words, 'Here is your scarab.' This experience punctured the desired hole in her rationalism and broke the ice of her intellectual resistance. The treatment could now be continued with satisfactory results.[26]

It is easy to see that the coincidence Jung reports here is relatively more meaningful than the one in which the same sequence of numbers is repeated first on a tram ticket, then on a theater ticket, and then in a phone number, for it marked a turning point in his relation with the patient and actually caused a solution to a problem in his professional life. In addition to that, though, it was uncanny, in the same way as the other example. What is uncanny about coincidences is that there is a noticeably significant connection between events where there is clearly no causal connection between them.

The causal connections between events are the ones that we learn through experience and that we can investigate scientifically in order to understand in more detail. This is what gives us the kind of knowledge we need in order to survive and to flourish with increasing powers of prediction and control of events. But there is also another kind of connection: one between a person and an event. A person can intentionally bring about an event that otherwise would not have happened. Of course, there is nothing miraculous about this; we don't thereby disrupt the cause-and-effect relations of nature. A person can only bring about an event by working with those cause-and-effect relations. Because we have the ability to act on things in this way, relations are set up between events and other events and between events and ourselves, in addition to the cause-and-effect relations between events. We might call them "relations of meaning."

In writing this book, for example, I am bringing about events that otherwise wouldn't take place, from marks appearing on paper to thoughts appearing in other people's minds (hopefully). There are cause-and-effect relations between those events, but there are also relations of meaning between them. The reason why certain marks appear rather than others is not just that certain events have taken place in my brain and that these are causally connected in a long chain with the appearance of those marks. For a full explanation we have to refer to the meaning of those events in my brain. Otherwise, we can't explain why it matters that those events rather than some others took place, for better or worse. The valid distinction between scribbling and writing depends on the meaningfulness of writing as contrasted to scribbling.

We more or less constantly take for granted our ability to act in and on the world in this way, even though we are sometimes frustrated by the limits of the cause-and-effect relations between events and are sometimes delighted by our mastery of them. What sometimes takes us by surprise is that the meaningful connections between events don't always depend on any conscious action of ours or of anyone else's. What happens when we notice a coincidence is that we notice a connection between events of the type that is normally produced only by the intentional intervention of a person. It isn't that one of the events causes the other. It's as if someone had brought about a meaningful connection between the events deliberately to create a commentary on something of significance to us; but we know we didn't do it, and it is also highly improbable that anyone else did.

Unlike Jung, who has quite a collection of actual examples of synchronicity in his essay, I find it hard to remember specific examples from my own experience, so I'm going to describe a fictional one that is like the kind of thing that I remember having experienced without remembering specific ones that make good examples. Suppose I had told my wife that I had "turned the table" on a difficult person at work, and jokingly remark that I now lead him around like a bull with a ring in his nose. At that very moment a commercial comes on TV with a shot of bulls rampaging through the streets of Pamplona. My comment didn't cause the commercial writers to come up with that image nor did it cause the commercial to appear at that time; and the commercial writers weren't intending to make a commentary on my remark. Nevertheless, both my wife and I notice it as if it were such a commentary, as evidenced when we look at each other with amused surprise.

Coincidences are remarkable because, while we habitually take for granted our ability to impose our intentions on the world in the small ways in which we are able, it happens less frequently that the relations of meaning between events take on their own life, so to speak, as commentaries on our own thoughts and actions, independently of our intentions. They are reminders that the goal is not to control everything but rather to interact with those forces that are outside one's control. They also constitute positive evidence of the meaningfulness of life. The more open one is to noticing coincidences, no matter how minor, the more often they occur, much in the way that paying attention to dreams one has at night results in more frequently remembered, and more richly detailed ones. Synchronicity makes life musical.

This is what I meant by "tuning in to the meaningfulness of life." One must avoid the temptation to invent a magical, pseudo-causal connection to explain coincidences. Resisting that temptation makes the difference between simply being alert to coincidences and being superstitious. This is a very important difference, because being alert to coincidences enriches one's life and shows that meaningfulness springs up like life itself, while being superstitious leads away from true religion by erecting a pretense of control where there is none.

Chapter 7

Individualistic Religion and Indeterminist Free Will

How much are we in control?

When I explain my own behavior by stating the beliefs and desires that motivated me to act, I do not normally imply that I could not have done otherwise.

John R. Searle[27]

Everything I've argued for so far depends on the fact, as I think it is, that we are in control of some things but that there are important things that are beyond our control. In this chapter, I want to make sure we're convinced that this is a fact.

Our old friend Epicurus gave us reasons to wonder whether there really are important things that are beyond our control. Death? 'Death is nothing to us. For what has been dispersed has no sensation. And what has no sensation is nothing to us.'[28] Suffering? It is beyond our powers to eliminate it completely, but that is not a problem:

Pain does not dwell continuously in the flesh. Extreme pain is present but a very brief time, and that which barely exceeds bodily pleasure continues no more than a few days. But chronic illness allows greater pleasure than pain in the flesh.[29]

Will I be loved? Epicurus talks about friendship rather than love, and he thinks it is important, all right, but not beyond our control. We just have to be wise:

Of all the things that wisdom provides for living one's entire life in happiness, the greatest by far is the possession of friendship.[30]

Will I go crazy? If I am right that this turns out to be the fear of having unpleasant thoughts that are false and the fear of feeling unpleasant emotions that are irrational (see Chapter 5), then Epicurus would say as I do that this is something we can learn to bring under our control. In fact, it is the whole point of philosophy:

Vain is the word of a philosopher by which no mortal suffering is healed. Just as medicine confers no benefit if it does not drive away bodily disease, so is philosophy useless if it does not drive away the suffering of the mind.[31]

And yet, some people are crazy, some are unloved, and I must confess that I'm afraid of dying and of suffering, and I have had my moments of anxiety, even panic and depression. More importantly, although philosophy certainly helps, and I'm all for it - it's my profession after all - my better moments haven't come as a result of my being in control of everything important, but rather as a result of everything important taking care of itself.

Epicurus doesn't address anxiety about meaninglessness, other than by expressing disapproval of suicide:

He is a little man in every way, for whom there are many persuasive reasons for departing from life.[32]

I agree with that statement wholeheartedly; but by simply taking for granted the meaningfulness of life, Epicurus overlooks the fact that if one really were in control of everything that matters, then the only way in which one could make life interesting and meaningful would be to give up some of that control. It is clear to me that if I ever was in control of everything that matters, then I must have decided to give up some of it and to forget that I ever had such total control, because I certainly don't have it now and don't remember ever having had it. For example, I am not in control of whether or not someone else loves me; and in fact it would be impossible to be in control of that, because if I could control it, then it would really be my own love for myself and not the love of someone else for me.

So, I don't think we should be convinced by Epicurus that we are in control of everything that matters.

From One Extreme to the Other

The extreme opposite is to believe that we aren't really in control of anything. Oddly, both literal theistic and scientistic[33] thinking have led to this conclusion. This is not to say that all theistic literalists and all devotees of scientism come to this conclusion. Some do, and some do not. But it will be just as instructive to see how and why some try to avoid the conclusion as it will be to understand why others embrace it. The literal theistic version begins with the premise that everything that happens is due to God's will and that is why God has foreknowledge. The scientistic version starts from the premise that everything that happens is due to natural laws and existing conditions, and that is why everything has a scientific explanation.

The literal theistic version proceeds as follows: as evidenced by God's promises and threats reported in the Bible, which never fail to come true, everything that happens is due to God's will and that is why He has foreknowledge. If God knows that someone is going to do a certain thing at a certain time, it is not possible for that person to do anything different at that time. But for every possible action anyone is going to take at any time, God does know what that person is going to do, and wills that it be done in that way. Otherwise, God would not be all-knowing and all-powerful. Therefore, when we think we are faced with a choice between two or more equally possible alternatives, we are wrong.

Only one of those alternatives is really possible: the one that God foresees and wills. Therefore, nothing is really under our control.[34]

The scientistic version runs along the following lines: There are natural laws that can be discovered and formulated precisely as equations, for example Newton's formulation of the law of gravity and Einstein's formulation of the relation between energy, mass, and the speed of light. The laws themselves are not necessary truths. It is conceivable that they could have been different, and if they had been, then the universe would have been drastically different. But what is necessary is that given the laws as they are, and given any particular set of conditions at a particular time and place, any change in those conditions will be precisely in accordance with the natural laws. Since the laws govern the motions of every particle of matter in the universe, and since our brains and bodies are masses made up of particles of matter, the motions of our brains and bodies are also subject to the laws. Therefore, since we can't change the natural laws and since we can't alter the past, there is always only one possible way in which our brains and bodies will move at any particular time. In order for us really to be in control of anything, it would have to be up to us how we move our brains and bodies. But since there is only one possible way that our brains and bodies can move at any particular time, it isn't up to us. Therefore, we aren't really in control of anything.

One tempting response to each of these arguments is to say that it doesn't matter whether or not the conclusion, that we aren't in control of anything, really follows from those premises, either the theistic or the scientistic ones, because we can't know what God knows or what a possessor of complete scientific knowledge would know; and so, practically speaking, it will always seem to us that we are in control of some things. However, this is no way to deal with anxiety about meaninglessness. If our problem is a worry that life is meaningless, and we have reasoned that a necessary condition for its meaningfulness is for us to be in control of some things but not of everything; then it is laughably inadequate to try to reassure ourselves by saying, 'Well, after all, it will always seem to us that we are in control of some things, and so it will always seem to us that life is meaningful.'

We need to convince ourselves either 1) that the conclusion that we aren't in control of anything doesn't really follow from either the theistic or the scientistic premises, or else 2) that, although the conclusion does follow from the premises, the premises themselves are false. Successfully prosecuting either of these strategies would eliminate these reasons for doubting that we are really in control of anything. However, this wouldn't give us any positive reason we don't already have, to believe that we are in control of some things. To achieve that result, we need a comparison of the alternative hypotheses about our control, or lack of it, that shows why we have more reason to believe that we are in control of some things than to believe that nothing is really under our control.

Determinism and Compatibilism

In order to clear the way for examining the alternative hypotheses, I need to explain some terminology and the connection between the theistic literalist and the scientistic versions. "Determinism" is the name for the following view: Given the laws of nature and the history of the universe up to any given moment (whether these are due to God's will or to the evolution of a blind, indifferent universe), there is only one possible thing that can happen next. As I noted above, it seems odd that a believer in theistic literalism and a believer in scientism can agree on such a fundamental question as whether or not we are really in control of anything. One thing that makes this seem less surprising is the reflection that a theist doesn't deny that there are the kind of uniform regularities we call natural laws. The theistic and the scientistic versions differ only as to whether the invariable, universal physical relations we call natural laws are due to God's will or whether, instead, the natural laws themselves are the ultimate explanatory factors.

In the theistic version God has foreknowledge of everything that happens because God wills everything that happens, from His creation of the universe with the particular initial conditions and the particular set of natural laws He has chosen to institute, to the unfolding of natural and human history. God could have chosen not to create the universe. He could have chosen a different set of initial conditions or a different set of natural laws. It is also within His power to change the natural laws whenever He wishes, either temporarily or permanently: temporarily in the case of miracles, permanently in the case of the transformation that will take place on Judgment Day. On this view scientific prediction works because we can discover the natural laws and apply them to explain the change from an observed set of conditions at one time and place to the set of conditions at another time and place, whether observed or not. If it doesn't work, that is either because of our carelessness - the usual cause - or, more rarely, because it is one of the times when God has changed the laws. In the latter case, the fact that our scientific expectations have been disappointed pales in significance compared to the fact that God has intervened.

The scientistic version simply deletes all reference to God in this account, with the result that there is actually no one who has foreknowledge of everything that happens. However, if there were someone who knew, like God, all the natural laws and all the details of the conditions at any given place and moment in the history of the universe, she or he could predict, or retrodict, the conditions of the universe at any other place and moment in the history of the universe. Scientific prediction works because, even without such god-like omniscience, it is possible to discover at least some of the natural laws (although the resulting theories are always open to revision in the light of future evidence) and it is possible to observe at least some of the conditions that hold at a particular place and time in the history of the universe.

As I said, not all theistic literalists nor all devotees of scientism believe that the conclusion follows that we are not in control of anything. That is, many of them attempt to follow the strategy of showing that even if the deterministic premises are true, we are still in control of some things. This view is called "compatibilism," because it is the belief that determinism and our control over some things are compatible. The theistic literalists who hold this view believe that the premises are true; but, because they think, as I do, that it is essential to true religion to believe that one is in control of some things but not of everything, they are motivated to find a reason to deny that the literalist view implies that we aren't in control of anything. In contrast, the compatibilists among the devotees of scientism take no position on whether the deterministic premises are true, but they do take a position that it is invalid to infer from those premises that we don't have control over anything. That is, they think that whether the correct scientific view turns out to be deterministic or indeterministic; either way, it can still be true that we are in control of some things.[35]

Where We Stand So Far

We have already seen a reason to doubt the theistic literalist premises, in the form of the God/universe problem. We would have to believe either that God is some unidentified part of the physical universe that created and controls all the rest, or else that God is a non-physical being who created and controls the physical universe. Either way, we have turned God's existence into a scientific hypothesis. On the first alternative, it is a wildly speculative one; and on the second, it is one that introduces an insoluble conceptual problem.

We also have reason to doubt the premises of the scientistic deterministic reasoning, as some of the devotees of scientism themselves admit. Our current best scientific theories tell us that what happens at the sub-atomic level is, in principle, predictable only statistically, and that there is no way of being sure that the indeterminism that exists at the subatomic level doesn't infect the macroscopic world as well.

So, it might seem that we have the result we want. Since we have reasons to doubt the deterministic premises of both versions of the argument to the conclusion that we are not in control of anything, we are free to doubt that conclusion also. Well, we are free to doubt it and to believe, instead, that we really are in control of some things; but we haven't really gained any new reason beyond the reason we already have to believe it, which is that we all speak and act as if we have control over some things. An argument that is unsound because it has a false premise may still have a true conclusion. It could still be true that we aren't really in control of anything even if Biblical literalism and scientistic determinism are both false.

So, we don't really have the result we wanted, which was reassurance that it is true that we are in control of some things. However, we are pointed in the right direction. To get there, we also need to tackle the question of the validity of the arguments. That is, supposing it is true that everything that happens is the result of God's immutable will, would it also have to be true that nothing is under our control? And, supposing it is true that natural laws plus existing conditions always determine what happens next, must it also be true that nothing is really up to us? According to compatibilism, the correct answer to both questions is No.

Since my announced goal is reassurance that we really do have control over some things, it may seem surprising that I'm going to argue that compatibilism is false; since according to compatibilism, we can consistently believe we have control over some things even if the premises of the deterministic arguments are true. However, I'm convinced that compatibilism is an evasion that causes one to relax one's guard against the deterministic premises. The deterministic premises really are incompatible with the conclusion that we have control over anything. I propose that we can find some reassurance that we really do have control over some things in the way that is a necessary condition for meaningfulness and morality, by seeing what is wrong with compatibilist reasoning. Let's call the denial of determinism "indeterminism," and the denial of compatibilism "incompatibilism." We might as well use the classic term "free will" also, as the name for our ability, if we have it, to control some things. Let's see if we can defend the thesis that we have indeterminist free will against compatibilist objections.

Incompatibilism

According to the compatibilist view, to say an action is free just means that if the agent had desired to do otherwise, he or she would have. But if determinism is true, it is never going to be the case that the agent will desire to do otherwise than either God's will or the laws of nature plus existing conditions determine. So, the incompatibilist reasons, since no one but God has control over what God wills, since no one but God has the power to alter the laws of nature, and since no one has the power to change the past, then, if determinism is true, then in any situation, at any moment, there is only one possible thing that can happen next. That is, if determinism is true, only God or nature ever has control over what happens next. Determinism is incompatible with our having control over anything. If we do have control over anything, determinism must be false.

There are two basic compatibilist responses. I don't think either one is convincing, but we need to understand them in order to be clear about the alternative hypotheses on offer. The first objection is to accuse the incompatibilist of committing a kind of fallacy that logicians call a "modal fallacy." The second objection is to argue that if an event is not determined, either by God's will or by the natural laws operating on existing conditions, then the only alternative is that it is a random, chance event, and that, surely, is not what anyone has in mind when they think of an action as being under one's control. A second way of expressing the second objection is to say that if incompatibilism is true, then a free choice would be a mystery, with no possible explanation.

The "Modal Fallacy" Objection

The first of these two objections sounds rather technical, and it is; but it is worth the trouble of understanding it to see what a desperate evasion compatibilism turns out to be.[36] First, we need to know what a modal fallacy is.[37] When we say that a statement must be true, or that it is necessarily true, we are clearly saying more than simply that it is true. Likewise, when we say that something could be true, or that it is possible, we are saying something less than that it actually is true. We can also talk about a statement being necessarily false, which is more than saying simply that it is false. That is, there are different ways or modes in which we can consider the truth or the falsity of a claim. Logicians use the term "modal statement" for a claim about the possibility or the necessity of something being true, or of something being false. Some examples are:

It is possible that the thief entered through the front door, if he had a key.
It is necessarily true that either the thief entered through the front door or he didn't.
If you had the money in the first place, then there must be something that happened to it.

An argument in which at least one of the premises or the conclusion is a modal statement is referred to as a "modal argument." A modal argument that is deceptively persuasive, that seems to be valid but isn't, is called a "modal fallacy."

Here is an example of a modal fallacy. It is a simple matter of logic or arithmetic that if my son Stan has two children, then he necessarily has at least one child. It is also true, not as a matter of logic but as a matter of fact, that Stan does have two children. It now seems to follow, again as a matter of simple logic, that he necessarily has at least one child. However, that conclusion is false. He does, in fact, have at least one child, but that isn't a necessary truth, since it is possible that he might never have had any children, and a necessary truth is one that couldn't possibly have been false.

What has gone wrong? What is wrong is that in our first premise:

If Stan has two children, then he necessarily has at least one child the "modal operator" (in this example the word "necessarily") appears to modify the "then" clause of the conditional "If. . ., then. . ." statement; when logically it really modifies the entire conditional statement. That is, what is being claimed to be not only true but necessarily true is the conditional statement that if Stan has two children, then he has at least one. So, the first premise can be clarified by stating it as:

Necessarily, if Stan has two children, then he has at least one. Then, when we add the second premise:

Stan has two children.

we get the proper conclusion:

Stan has at least one child.

and we avoid the fallacy of concluding that he necessarily has at least one child.

The first objection to incompatibilism says that incompatibilist reasoning also involves a modal fallacy. (For ease of exposition, in what follows, I will use the scientistic version of determinism, on the understanding that we could get the theistic version by adding the assumption that the laws of nature and the history of the world are due to God's will.) The charge is that the modal fallacy occurs when the incompatibilist reasons as follows:

1) If determinism is true, then, if the laws of nature are as they are in our actual universe, and if the past history of the universe is as it is up to the present moment, then there is only one possible thing that can happen next, that is, whatever happens next happens necessarily.
2) The past history of the world and the laws of nature are as they are at the present moment.
3) Therefore, if determinism is true, there is only one possible thing that can happen next.
4) Therefore, determinism is incompatible with there being more than one possible future.

According to the compatibilist, this argument is invalid. Determinism is compatible with there being more than one possible future, and what is wrong with the incompatibilist argument is the same thing that was wrong with the modal fallacy about Stan and the number of his children. The modal operator ("only one possible thing" = "necessarily") applies to the entire conditional in the first premise and not just to its consequent. What is necessary according to determinism is the causal dependence of what happens next on whatever has gone before and the laws of nature. This is not the claim that the past could not possibly have been different, nor that the laws of nature in the actual universe could not possibly have been different, nor that there is only one possibility for what happens next. So, the compatibilist can maintain that it is necessary that if the past and the laws are a certain way, then one certain thing will happen next; and he can consistently deny that there is only one possible thing that can happen next.[38]

Reply to the Objection

Our imaginary compatibilist is right about the modal fallacy but wrong that this is going to settle the matter in favor of compatibilism. There is such a mistake, as the simple example of Stan and the number of his children makes clear, and an incompatibilist who argues as above that determinism implies that there is only one possible future would be committing such a fallacy. However, as an incompatibilist I can reply as follows: I admit that determinism doesn't imply that there is only one possible future and thus no freedom of choice, but it does imply something else that is hard to believe. It implies that when I make a choice between two or more different possible futures, I am also making a choice between two or more different possible pasts or between two or more different sets of natural laws.

Let's take a simple example to help make this clear. Suppose I'm about to decide whether to wear a blue shirt or a white shirt. If determinism is true, then, given the laws of nature and the relevant facts in the history of the universe up to that moment, only one of these apparent possibilities (I choose the blue shirt or I choose the white one) is really possible. It may be that neither I nor anyone else knows which one it is until my hand reaches out for one rather than the other, but that doesn't matter. The fact remains that only one of these alternatives is consistent with the causal history leading up to this moment, and so it isn't up to me which shirt I'm going to wear. I'm going to wear whichever one I am caused to "choose."

Now, suppose the compatibilist responds by saying, 'No. Don't you see? This is just like the modal fallacy of concluding that Stan necessarily has at least one child from the premises: 1) that it is necessarily true that if he has two, he has at least one, and 2) that he does have two. It doesn't follow that it's necessarily true that he has at least one. It only follows that he does have at least one. Likewise, from the premises: 1) that it's necessarily true that if the laws of nature and the history of the universe are a certain way, then you'll pick, let's say, the blue shirt, and 2) that the laws of nature and the history of the universe are that way; it doesn't follow that it's necessarily true that you'll pick the blue shirt. It only follows that you will pick the blue shirt.' I would respond by acknowledging that it isn't necessarily true that Stan has at least one child nor that I will choose the blue shirt. That is, it could be false that Stan has at least one child, and it could be false that I will choose the blue shirt. However, if it were false that Stan has at least one child (because he didn't have any), then at least one of the premises would also have to be false. Either it would have to be false that it's necessarily true that if he has two, he has at least one; or, it would have to be false that he does have two children. Since the first premise is arithmetically true, it would have to be that the second premise is false. In other words, to state the obvious: if Stan didn't have any children, he wouldn't have two of them. So, yes, it's just as possible that he might not have had any children as it is that he had at least one, but it isn't possible that he didn't have any, *and* that he had two. Similarly, if I didn't choose the blue shirt, then either it would have to be false that it's necessarily true that if the laws of nature and the history of the universe are a certain way, then I will choose the blue shirt; or, it would have to be false that the laws of nature and the history of the universe are that certain way. Since to give up the first premise is to give up determinism, and since the compatibilist is arguing that determinism is compatible with a real choice; it would have to be the second premise that is false. That is to say, we have to suppose that if I choose the white shirt (so that it is false that I chose the blue shirt), then it would also have to be false that the laws of nature and the history of the universe up to that point were as specified. Something about either one or the other or both would have had to be different. In other words, the compatibilist hypothesis turns out to be that determinism is compatible with real choice because when a person makes a choice, he or she is not only choosing one particular action over another, but is also choosing one set of natural laws or one prior history.

Three Hypotheses

Now, as far as I can tell it is conceptually possible that whenever I do make a choice between alternative possible futures, as I think I often do, I am also making a choice between possible pasts and/or natural laws. In fact, the hypothesis that this is what happens is irrefutable, because there is no way of checking whether or not it is true. If the past or a law of nature gets altered, then of course all available evidence will show that that is the way it was all along. However, as the late British philosopher, Karl Popper, has argued, although all philosophical hypotheses are irrefutable, in the sense that there is no possible empirical counterexample to them, it doesn't follow that they are all true. They can't all be true, since some of them contradict each other. Neither does it follow that we can't find good reasons for preferring one philosophical hypothesis over another.[39]

Let's compare three philosophical hypotheses about determinism and free will. The first one is compatibilist determinism, by which I mean the hypothesis that determinism is true; that is, there is a necessary causal dependence of what happens next on the laws of nature plus whatever has gone before; and yet we also do have free choices, because when we are choosing between alternative futures as to what happens next, we are also choosing between alternative sets of past histories and laws of nature.

The second hypothesis is incompatibilist determinism, that is that determinism is true, and further that there are no genuine alternative possibilities for any time: past, present, or future. According to this hypothesis, I can't alter the past and I can't really choose one alternative future rather than another. When I think that is what I'm doing, it is only because I don't then yet know which of what seem to be equally possible alternatives is the only possible one.

The third, and final, hypothesis I want to compare is that there is indeterminist free will. According to this hypothesis, once a possibility becomes actual, alternatives that had been really possible cease to be real possibilities any longer. This is the hypothesis, in other words, that determinism is false, and that although I am not free to choose between alternative pasts, I am free to choose between alternative futures.

Response to the "Sheer Chance or Mystery" Objection

Compatibilists typically criticize the hypothesis of indeterminist free will on the grounds that it involves a mystery as to how or why I can choose between alternative futures, given a fixed past. This is the second objection to incompatibilism that I want to address; namely, that it implies that if there is free will then determinism must be false and that this in turn implies that free choice is a matter of sheer chance or else simply a mystery with no explanation. If everything could have been exactly the same up to the moment of the free choice, no matter which one of two or more competing alternatives gets chosen, then what possible explanation could there be for the choice of the one rather than the other?

This objection is more serious than the "modal fallacy" objection, which saves compatibilism at the expense of requiring us to believe that we alter the past or the laws of nature every time we make a choice. However, there is a satisfactory defense of indeterminist free will against this objection, too. I'll try to explain it in terms of an example discussed by Robert Kane: A woman is on her way to a business meeting that is crucial to her career, when she sees someone being mugged in an alley. If she stops to call the police or otherwise tries to help the victim, she will be late for the meeting and her career will be harmed. If she doesn't stop, her conscience will bother her. As Kane points out, whichever decision she makes, there will be an explanation, either in terms of her prudential, career interests or in terms or her moral motives. We are supposing that both of these competing motives are part of the prior conditions, and so we can believe that whichever of the two alternative possible futures that she chooses, the prior conditions can remain the same and still yield an explanation.[40]

The critic is likely to remain unsatisfied by this, however, and might reply as follows. We must suppose either that it was already true, before the woman made her decision, that one of her competing motives dominated the other one, or else that her making the decision retroactively makes one of her competing motives dominate the other; because if we don't, then we won't really have an explanation as to why she made the decision that she did. In other words, we are tacitly adopting either incompatibilist determinism: that determinism is true and since no one can alter the past, there is only one possible future, or else compatibilist determinism: that determinism is true but that there is a free choice between really possible alternative futures because there is a corresponding choice between really possible alternative pasts. On the hypothesis of indeterminist free will: that determinism is false and so there can be a free choice between alternative futures while holding the past fixed; then her choice cannot be explained in terms of one of her motives being stronger than the other. This is because this hypothesis commits us to the claim that she is free to decide one way or the other no matter which of her motives was stronger prior to her decision.

The objection is that an explanation of the woman's action must link that action to facts about prior conditions and also predict that she will act similarly if and when similar circumstances arise in the future. So, if we hold that she can freely act one way or the other with no corresponding change in the prior conditions, then we have no such explanation.

The answer to this objection is to explain how it can be that the indeterminist free will hypothesis can allow for such an explanation. Consider the case in which the woman decides to stop and call the police. The woman's action can be explained by saying that, since she decided to sacrifice her career interests in order to do what she thought she was morally obligated to do, her motivation to do her moral duty was probably stronger than her motivation to further her career in this instance. The "probably" is called for because it could be that her competing motives were equally strong and she decided on doing the moral thing rather than the prudential thing simply because she knew she had to do one or the other. She could just as well have decided to go on to the business meeting without stopping. Sometimes we do just make a choice without any dominating reason to choose one thing rather than another. For example, a magician prompts you to 'pick a card, any card,' and you pick one without having any stronger motivation to pick that card than you do to pick any other.[41] The theorist who adopts the hypothesis that there is indeterminist free will has no difficulty accepting this possibility. By contrast, a theorist who adopts either version of determinism, compatibilist or incompatibilist, will have to say that there must be an explanation in terms of prior conditions, even if there doesn't seem to be any.

The crucial question is whether or not the believer in indeterminist free will is able to offer any explanation other than "She just chose that way" in cases where a pattern of behavior seems to establish that one competing motive dominated another. The answer is Yes, and there is nothing complicated or mysterious about the explanation. If, in our example, the woman chooses to ignore the incident in the alley and keep her business appointment, and there is evidence in her past of making similar choices in similar situations and she goes on to reinforce this evidence by her future behavior, the believer in indeterminist free will is perfectly free to say that she chose to keep her business appointment because her prudential motives dominated her moral motives.

However, the believer in indeterminist free will is stuck with a theoretical commitment that is like the determinist's commitment turned inside out. Where the determinist is obligated to say that, even when there is no evidence for any feature in the prior conditions that necessitated the choice, there nevertheless must be some such feature; the indeterminist is obligated to say that, even when there is plenty of evidence that a choice was made because of some feature of the prior conditions, nevertheless a different choice could have been made, even given exactly the same prior conditions. Otherwise, it wasn't a free choice on the incompatibilist, indeterminist view I am elucidating here.

Reasons for Preferring the Indeterminist Commitment

We have a good reason, though, to prefer the indeterminist commitment over the determinist one. If a person makes a choice for a good reason, then it makes sense to cite that reason as an explanation. It would be theoretically undesirable, though, to hold that, given that reason, the person had no choice, for then it would be difficult to explain why sometimes people have more reason to choose A than to choose B, and know that they do, and yet go ahead and choose B anyway. We can explain cases of extremely poor decision-making in terms of psychological compulsions, or the effects of social conditioning and the like, by contrasting them with free decisions based on good reasons. However, we also need to be able to explain what happens when a person makes a good choice despite the fact that there is just as much evidence for psychological compulsion or social conditioning as in a case where such compulsion or conditioning is the explanation for why a person couldn't help but make a bad "choice." On the theory that there is indeterminist free will, the explanation is that prior conditions never constitute jointly sufficient conditions for a choice. The theory doesn't commit us to the claim that everything that appears to be a choice really is one, i.e., the claim that there are no genuine cases of psychological or social conditioning causing compulsive behavior. It allows us to make distinctions between real and apparent choice and between real and apparent compulsion, by observing a person's actions over a sufficiently long period of time, whether that person is oneself or someone else.

By contrast, on the theory that there are always prior conditions that are sufficient for the occurrence of any event, we are committed to either 1) the claim that the possibility that any event could have failed to transpire or been replaced by some other event is the possibility that those prior conditions were also different, or else 2) the claim that the actual history of the universe is the only possible one.

On the first of these alternatives, the explanation for what happens when a person makes a good choice despite the fact that there is just as much evidence for psychological conditioning or social conditioning as in a similar bad "choice" case, is that there must be some relevant undetected difference between the two cases in the prior conditions. It won't matter at all if, despite a diligent search, we are never able to find any evidence that would enable us to say what the difference is. The theory of compatibilist determinism entails a metaphysical commitment that different choices have different prior conditions.

On the second alternative, that the actual universe is the only possible universe, the explanation is that the illusion of choice is always a matter of our ignorance of some of the factors constituting the sufficient conditions for an event, so there is nothing special about a case in which a person makes a good "choice" in spite of evidence for psychological compulsion or social conditioning. This may show that we didn't have enough evidence to establish exactly what the causal links were; but even in cases where we can't find evidence for the causal links, there is, by hypothesis, some underlying set of sufficient conditions that compels in every case.

The good reason, then, to prefer the indeterminist commitment over the determinist one is that indeterminism turns out to be more sensitive to empirical evidence than determinism is. Admittedly, the hypothesis that there is indeterminist free will commits us to the claim that, even when there is plenty of evidence that a choice was made because of some feature of the prior conditions, nevertheless a different choice could have been made. However, whenever it happens that someone surprises us by acting in a way we didn't expect, we can then take this case as a significant piece of evidence to be correlated with existing evidence in a new theory that attempts to explain the person's motives and behavior. By contrast, both versions of determinism commit us to claims that are simply immune to evidence.

Summary

To sum up, then, each of the three hypotheses: compatibilist determinism, incompatibilist determinism, and indeterminist free will, is irrefutable; but noting the implications of each, we can find good reasons for preferring one over the other two, namely the hypothesis that there is a kind of free will that is incompatible with determinism. So finally, we have not only good reasons to believe that deterministic arguments are unsound, but also a positive reason to believe that we do have control over some things, in addition to the reason we already had, which was that we all speak and act as if we have control over some things. Once again, both theistic literalism and scientism are operating on the premises of a false dilemma. It is just as false that we must choose between what William James called "iron block determinism," on the one hand, or sheer chance, on the other, as it is that we must choose between a literal creator God or a blind, pitiless, indifferent universe.[42] Ours is a universe in which love and free choice and moral responsibility are central because it contains caring human beings, who are in control of some things but who are not in control of everything. In particular, they are not in control of some things that are very important to them, a situation they intelligently symbolize as the fear of God and the trust in God, with the latter dominant.

Chapter 8

Salvation and Control

Are we in control of our own salvation?

But the highest passion in a human being is faith, and here no generation begins other than where its predecessor did, every generation begins from the beginning, the succeeding generation comes no further than the previous one, provided the latter was true to its task and didn't betray it.

Kierkegaard, in Fear and Trembling[43]

As we saw in the previous chapter, we have good reasons to believe that Epicurus was wrong in holding that only unimportant things are outside our control, and we have good reasons to believe that we can decide, in some ways, what happens next. But could it be that our situation turns out to be like that described by Epicurus, only turned inside out? Could it be that only unimportant things are under our control? If so, then even though we still would have good reasons to reject a thoroughgoing determinism, it wouldn't really matter. We may as well be determinists if our free actions can only affect trivial matters. We need to know which important things, if any, are under our control, and which are not.

Is it under our control whether or not we are prudent, that is, whether we make intelligent, well informed decisions, taking into account our own long-term self-interest, or whether instead we carelessly act without worrying about the consequences? Epicurus could be right in thinking that it is up to each of us to make wise decisions rather than foolish ones, while he is wrong to think that that is all that matters. What else matters? There are two important areas where the teachings of Epicurus are inadequate: morality and salvation.

Epicurus' treatment of morality consists of his explanations of the importance of pleasure, of friendship, and of justice. Pleasure is important because it is the standard for judging every good. He holds that genuine pleasure is 'freedom from bodily pain and mental anguish.' It is not 'the pleasure of profligates or that which lies in sensuality, as some ignorant persons think.'[44] Friendship is important, on his view, because the most likely threat any of us faces is not from natural disasters, which are relatively rare, or from non-human predators, whom we can easily outsmart, but from other human beings. Friends are those who wish us good rather than harm. By cultivating friendship and avoiding making enemies, we can secure the greatest freedom from fear of being harmed by others.[45] He explains justice as a sort of pact one makes with other people not to harm them, in exchange for their promise not to harm one's self. He holds that the reason a wise person will never do anything unjust is because of the realization that one can never be free of the anxiety that one will be caught and harmed in retribution.[46] What he leaves unexplained is why we have a conception of morality as motivated by concern for doing the right thing, independently of whether or not this furthers or harms one's own non-moral interests.

As for salvation, what is inadequate about Epicurus' view on whether or not everything is fundamentally all right is not that he holds that there is anything fundamentally wrong, but rather that his conception of "allrightness" depends on our being in control of everything important. Such a conception is inadequate in any situation in which one finds that something important is happening that is not under one's control.

I still haven't answered the question whether being prudent is under our control. If it is, then why is anyone ever foolish? Surely, the wise decision would be to choose to be wise. So, the wise wisely choose to be wise, and the foolish foolishly choose to be foolish. But then it wouldn't really be a matter of choice since, by definition, a wise person would not make a foolish decision (for then he or she would not be wise, but foolish), and a foolish person would not make a wise choice. But we know this is wrong. The solution is that no one is immutably wise or immutably foolish. Those who are generally wise are capable of making foolish mistakes, and those who are generally foolish are capable of making wise decisions. But if everyone is capable of being wise and capable of being foolish, what determines which it is going to be? Since we have decided we have better reasons to believe in indeterminist free will than in either compatibilist or incompatibilist determinism, the answer is that, except for genuine cases of psychological compulsion, such as neurosis or drug addiction, it is the individual self who freely determines it. Furthermore, it is surely better strategy to assimilate cases of psychological compulsion to cases of making a free choice, whether foolish or wise, than it would be to assimilate cases of making wise or foolish decisions to cases of psychological compulsion. One important element in curing addiction or neurosis is for the sufferer to take responsibility for her or his condition. So yes, the choice between being prudent and being foolish is one of the important things that are under our control.

What about morality, and what about the most important thing of all: salvation, or the realization that everything is fundamentally all right? This is the question that Erasmus and Luther debated, except, of course, that they would describe salvation as being chosen by God to have eternal life and everlasting joy.

One of the problems with the original Christian view is that it seems unfair of God to damn some of his creatures to everlasting torment while choosing others to receive everlasting joy. However, the Athanasian creed says that believing that God does this is a necessary condition for being saved.[47] The free-will defense against the problem of evil could be used as a justification for God's damnation of evil doers. The argument would be that although this seems unfair, it is better than the only alternative, which would be to deny free will to everyone by creating automatic good-doing machines instead of human beings. I've already pointed out one problem with that justification, which is that the limited ability of a human being to do evil cannot cause him or her to deserve unlimited punishment.

Luther saw another problem with a free-will justification of Christian salvation-or-damnation. Those who hope that they are among the saved, which includes everyone who is not so blind as not to realize what is at stake, may be tempted to think that it is by their own free will that they can be the kind of person whom God will choose to reward with eternal joy. That is, if the damned get their punishment because they deserve it, it seems reasonable to think that the saved get their reward because they deserve it. But if people were capable of freely choosing to do God's will, thus ensuring themselves a place among the saved, then it wouldn't have been necessary for Jesus to die for our sins, and it would be irrelevant that Jesus was crucified.[48] So Luther argued that, on our own, we are powerless to do anything that leads to our salvation. Whenever we do act in such a way that leads to our salvation, it is not we ourselves who act through our own free will. Rather, it is the Holy Spirit acting through us.

Erasmus agreed that God's grace is necessary for salvation, but he argued that unless free will is also a factor, then the frequent exhortations and admonitions found in the Bible would be pointless. Luther replied that the threats 'are for the purpose of instruction and illumination, to teach us what we ought to do and show us that we cannot do it'[49] without the help of the Holy Spirit; and the promises of reward are to encourage us 'to go forward, persevere, and conquer in doing good and enduring evil,' which we can do through 'the power and operation of the Holy Spirit.'[50] Luther insisted, above all, that the reward that is promised is not the consequence of merit. It is not something that we can earn through our own efforts.

Erasmus worried that Luther's denial that free will plays any role in salvation would lead the common people to reason that they are free to act as immorally as they choose, since choosing to act morally wouldn't make any difference as to whether or not they are among the saved.[51] Luther responded that, on the contrary, it is Erasmus's view that undermines true morality. To hold that salvation is the reward for acting morally makes morality a selfish choice.[52]

Since we aren't even sure that we hope we will all be resurrected on Judgment Day, we turn to a conception of salvation that we are sure we hope to attain: the realization that everything is fundamentally all right. We turn also to a conception of morality consistent with that conception of salvation: that moral actions are those that give us all good reasons to believe that everything is fundamentally all right, and that immoral actions do the opposite. Then, given our conclusion from the previous chapter that we have more reason to believe in indeterminist free will than in either incompatibilist or compatibilist determinism, we should agree with Erasmus that it is within our power to choose to act morally rather than immorally. However, Luther is right to criticize the view that one should act morally in order to earn the reward of being saved. Rather, the more a person chooses to act morally, the better reason we have to think she or he is saved.

A person who is not at least partially persuaded that everything is fundamentally all right has no reason to choose to do the decent thing; because if there is something fundamentally wrong with the way things are, then doing the right thing, whether in some signal act of self-sacrifice and heroism or in the small things of daily life, won't fix it. So why bother? The fact that you do bother shows that you do not think there is something fundamentally wrong with the way things are. Therefore, every small act of kindness, every little effort of self-discipline, is another piece of evidence that deep down you believe that everything is fundamentally all right.

Now, here is why Luther is right and Erasmus is wrong about free will and salvation. Believing that everything is fundamentally all right is a necessary condition for realizing that everything is fundamentally all right, but it is not sufficient. In addition, it must actually be true that everything is fundamentally all right, and it is not within anyone's power, except God's, to make it true. As I have argued, the best way to conceive of God is as a symbol of the fact that, although we are in control of some things, there are important things outside our control. The fear of God is the thorough realization of the seriousness of your utter helplessness in the face of things that are beyond your control and that you wish were not happening, such as an earthquake, or the sudden, unexpected death of someone you love. The trust in God is the faith that, deep down, it is still somehow all right. When I say that only God has the power to make it true that everything is fundamentally all right, I don't mean that now, contrary to what I've said before, I believe literally in God as either a physical or non-physical non-human person who created the physical universe and can destroy it whenever He wishes. That view simply makes God into a bad scientific hypothesis. What I mean is that you can realize that everything is fundamentally all right even though neither you nor anyone else, but only reality itself, makes it that way. It is a sacrilege to take credit for it, as if, unless you had realized it, it simply wouldn't have been true.

Although it is within our power to act morally, we know that we act immorally sometimes. Even if we have realized that everything is fundamentally all right, we don't always remember it in its full glory, and we don't always live up to it. It is pretty clear that if everyone acted immorally all the time, everything would not be fundamentally all right. It is also clear that if everyone had to act morally all the time in order for everything to be fundamentally all right, then we could hold out little hope of being saved.

As it is, many people act morally much of the time, and everything is fundamentally all right. But it is evidently not within anyone's power to act morally all the time, and it is not within anyone's power to make anyone else act morally, and it is not within anyone's power to make it true that everything is fundamentally all right. That is something to be thankful for, not to take credit for. Since it is impossible to realize something that is not true, it follows that we cannot be saved, that is, realize that everything is fundamentally all right, unless everything is fundamentally all right. Therefore, salvation, the most important thing of all, is not within our power. That doesn't imply that we can't have it, but only that it isn't our doing.

What of Luther's insistence that the life and crucifixion of Jesus were necessary for our salvation? One of the things I don't like about literalistic Christianity is the insistence on a literal acceptance that Jesus died for our sins, coupled with a fondness for the symbolism of bloody, ritualistic sacrifice inherited from ancient Judaism: that we are cleansed of our sins by being 'washed in the blood of the lamb.' Nevertheless, I think we can make sense of what is being symbolized in the story that Jesus, the Son of God, was subjected to a humiliating death, and that this led to the salvation of those who are worthy of it. Here is one part of what is symbolized: Jesus died because of our sins of misusing political power and of confusing the goal of politics with the goal of religion. Pontius Pilate misused his political power by imposing a humiliating death upon someone, and the chief priests made the horrible mistake of thinking that true religion may be defended by conspiring with the coercive powers of the state to eliminate those who are seen as a threat to religion. Jesus' resurrection symbolizes the real power of true religion, which has nothing to do with having control over other people. However, this is also symbolized just as well simply by His having suffered a humiliating death. He had already accomplished what He needed to accomplish, and His death did not wipe that out. The fact that His tormentors tried to make His death humiliating only dramatizes their sinfulness. There is more to the story than this, though.

Becoming thoroughly convinced that everything is fundamentally all right happens as a result of being confronted with existential anxiety: whatever it is that one thinks is the worst possible thing that can happen at that moment, and then finding that it turns into something better than one had ever imagined. This is symbolized in the Bible as being tested by God. Jesus' crucifixion and resurrection symbolize a fusion of God and humanity undergoing the test. What can be worse than killing God? And yet, even that turns out all right.

Except in the Preface, I have tried to avoid autobiography, but here I think it may be helpful to say that in my own life there are two types of experiences that have given me the deepest conviction that everything is fundamentally all right: psychedelic trips and undergoing (and recovering from) quadruple coronary artery bypass surgery. Overcoming existential anxiety is the common feature.[53] While recovering from that surgery, I was so very glad to be alive and wanted to tell everyone how beautiful the world was; but, at the same time, I knew that it would have been all right if I had died. That's because I was so appreciative of the value of life, including the life I had already lived. It would have been sheer greed to demand more, but I was certainly glad I was getting more. Another connection with Christianity that I have recently discovered as a result of reading Albert Schweitzer's *Quest of the Historical Jesus* is that having come of age during the height of the psychedelic revolution, as my friends and I thought of it then, helps me understand the spirit of the times when Jesus and his followers expected the imminent transformation of the world. Just as Christianity developed out of the necessity of dealing with the fact that the transformation didn't happen as expected, so we former hippies have had to deal with a similar situation.[54] The problem for modern Christians is reconciling the world-denying message of Jesus with their accommodations to our lovely world as it is. Similarly, the problem for us ex-hippies is to stay connected with the spiritually revolutionary implications of psychedelic experience while enjoying the advantages of what we used to call "the establishment," but which is just civilization-so-far.

The story of Jesus' ordeal is prefigured in the Bible by the story of God's testing of Abraham, which Kierkegaard used as the touchstone for his examination of the meaning of faith. Contrary to Kierkegaard's interpretation, I think Abraham is worthy of veneration as the father of faith only if he never had any intention of going through with the murder of his son. By outwardly following God's instructions right up to the last moment, when the next step would have been to cut Isaac's throat, he demonstrated his belief that God would back down. Then why did God say, when He stopped Abraham, that He did so because, "now I know that you fear God, since you have not withheld your son, your only son, from me"? (Gen. 22:12, NRSV) Surely, God would know not only Abraham's outward behavior but also his innermost thoughts and feelings. The text tells us, then, that Abraham did fear God as well as trust in Him. He feared that God might not stop him at the last minute. He feared that maybe the Judge of all the earth would do what is not just. After all, the Judge had already demonstrated, simply by imposing this test on Abraham in the first place, that He was capable of teetering on the brink of being the kind of god for whom the appropriate emotion is nothing but fear. Also, Abraham had already had to remind God of His justice and mercy in order to get Him to avoid killing the innocent along with the guilty when He destroyed Sodom, saying,

Far be it from you to do such a thing, to slay the righteous with the wicked, so that the righteous fare as the wicked! Far be that from you! Shall not the Judge of all the earth do what is just? (Gen. 18.25 NRSV)

However, God had also demonstrated his trustworthiness by keeping his promises to Abraham. The keeping of the promise that was most meaningful to Abraham was hanging in the balance as Abraham approached the mountain in the land of Moriah, where God had instructed him to offer up Isaac as a burnt offering. That was the promise that, through Isaac, Abraham would have descendants as numerous as the grains of dust, as the stars. Despite his fears, Abraham trusted that God would keep his promise. Faith is a combination of trust and fear, where the trust is stronger than the fear. If Abraham had known with certainty that God would back down at the last minute, then there would have been no need for faith. If Abraham had been overwhelmed by the fear that God was a crazy, unjust god, then there would have been no faith. Abraham undoubtedly experienced the anguish of trust battling fear. Trust won out and it turned out to be justified, and that is why Abraham is the father of faith. If God had not backed down, then none of us would be saved; that is, this would symbolize what, thankfully, is not true: that there is something fundamentally wrong with the way things are.

The story of the crucifixion and resurrection of Jesus is, in one way, like the Abraham and Isaac story, but with an alternate ending. The murder of the Son is carried out, but then He is miraculously restored to life. If this had been what had happened with Abraham and Isaac, however; then, despite the happy ending, Abraham would not have been the father of faith. If we suppose that Abraham had said to himself, 'God will keep His promise, so either He will stop me at the last minute or He will let me go ahead and kill Isaac and will then miraculously restore him to life,' and that this was what constituted his faith in God; then we would be wrong to admire him as the father of faith, even if God did still stop him at the last minute. For if that was what he thought, then he was willing to murder his son just because God told him to do it, and we should regard him as the father of those who murder their own children, not as the father of faith. Kierkegaard was right that faith transcends ethics, but wrong to think that this implies faith might require one to act immorally.[55] It transcends ethics in that one cannot earn salvation by choosing to act morally rather than immorally. But no one chooses to act immorally as a result of realizing that everything is fundamentally all right. One can't help but want to share that realization, and deliberately doing something morally wrong is precisely to give everyone a good reason to doubt one has realized any such thing. If God had required Abraham to murder Isaac and had then restored him to life, then God would be a cruel god, and something would be fundamentally wrong.

Someone might object that it was also cruel of God to put Abraham to the test and then back down at the last minute, so there would still be something fundamentally wrong. However, as long as we suppose that Abraham had faith that God would back down, although he was afraid that He wouldn't, but that in either case he was resolved not to murder his son; then the story represents the way any of us can be tested in the most severe way that is yet consistent with everything being fundamentally all right.[56]

Given what I've just written, how can it also be all right that in the case of Jesus, the Son was murdered and restored to life? Two significant differences are that the murderers were human beings whom we recognize as having acted immorally (and whom we certainly don't regard as fathers of faith) and that we are told that Jesus is the Son of God and is in fact God Himself in human form. What this represents is the fact that the worst thing one can imagine can't really happen. Sin is disrespecting, wasting the goodness that life brings. The doctrine of original sin just means that we all fall short of the opposite of sin, which would be something like being in a continual state of fully appreciating that goodness. To say that Jesus has saved us from our sins means that you can be saved in spite of your sins if you realize that the worst sin of all, which would be to destroy the source of goodness, is impossible. Goodness can take care of itself.

There is another important difference, between the case of Abraham and Isaac and the case of God the Father and Jesus. When God tested Abraham, He required him to respond to the demand that he, the individual human being, Abraham, be willing to give up what he held most dear, another individual human being, his beloved son Isaac, whose young life would be sacrificed to please God. In contrast, when God the Father willingly gave up his beloved son Jesus, the situation was reversed. It was God who was making the sacrifice for the benefit of each of us, as individuals.

Why did God do that? There are two different gospel songs with the same title, 'Who Am I?' that address this question. Who am I, that the Creator and Lord of the universe would sacrifice His only, beloved Son (Who is also Himself) so that I might have eternal life? It won't do to say that it was no real sacrifice, on the grounds that God the Father knew that God the Son would be resurrected, for Christian doctrine insists that Jesus was both fully divine and fully human, and the fully human Jesus really did suffer both physical and emotional torture and death, as evidenced in his final cry, 'My God, my God, why have you forsaken me?' (Mark 15.34) As Schweitzer points out, Jesus believed to the end that, despite the prophecies, it would have been possible for God the Father to have brought about the transformation without the prophesied preceding tribulation, and that is what he prayed for at Gethsemane. (Mark 14.32-36)[57] So, clearly, in Christianity it is no small matter that God makes this sacrifice and that it is for the benefit of each of us. What is being symbolized here is the importance of each of us, as an individual, not only in the egoistic way in which my concerns are especially important to me and yours are to you, and everyone else's are to him or to her, but also in the way in which each of us is important to those who love us. In Chapter 4, I addressed the question: how are we to conceive of God? In the next chapter, we need to ask: how are we to conceive of the individual human person?

Chapter 9

The Importance of the Individual (Part I)

Who Am I?

The human spirit is the lamp of the Lord,
searching every inmost part.

Proverbs 20.27 (NRSV)

One thing that is clear is that each of us has a first-person perspective, from which she or he can ask the question: who am I? A simple answer would be to state one's name, or to say something along the lines of, 'I am the person who . . . ,' where the blank is filled in by a description that is detailed enough to pick oneself out among the available candidates. Or, you could say, 'I am this person here,' or wave a hand or nod your head to indicate which person you are among all the persons there.

Of course, any of those responses would miss the point of the question asked in the gospel songs, 'Who Am I?' which is how it can be that God so loves little old me that He was willing to die for me. In the version of the song that Elvis Presley recorded, the lyric admits, 'The answer I may never know,' and in the version recorded by the Casting Crowns, in lyrics addressed to God, the answer is that 'I am a flower quickly fading. . . . A wave tossed in the ocean, a vapor in the wind,' but finally, 'I am yours.'[58]

There is a problem with the self-abasement part of this answer, though, which is that Genesis tells us that God created humankind in His image. (Gen. 1.27) Surely God is not a flower quickly fading, nor does He have the sort of dependent and evanescent existence of a wave tossed in the ocean or a vapor in the wind. So, if humankind was made in God's image, then each of us must not be completely like a fading flower, a wave, or a vapor. The last line, 'I am yours,' is perhaps meant to express that. We need to decide if it is true, as it says in the Elvis version, that "'The answer I may never know.'[59] Even God could ask, 'Who am I?' According to Jack Miles's persuasive interpretation in his biography of God, He discovers the answer to this question by doing things, by creating humankind in His own image, and then discovering that the experiment has its dangers, as when Adam and Eve eat the forbidden fruit and God worries,

> See the man has become like one of us, knowing good and evil; and now, he might reach out his hand and take also from the tree of life, and eat, and live forever. (Gen. 3.22 NRSV)

So, another feature that is essential to the concept of an individual, whether human or divine, is that a person does things and reveals, or discovers, his or her identity by doing them.

Since God is a symbol, of the fact that there are important things outside our control, and the symbol is the whole Biblical account of God, which includes the well-known passage that says God created us in his image, does it follow that we, too, are symbols? The answer must be a qualified, 'In a way, Yes, and in another way, No.' Like God, we, too, are symbols, inasmuch as we transcend ourselves by interacting meaningfully with each other, thus coming to personify, for good or bad, a particular combination of universal character traits. But unlike God, we also literally exist as physical beings in a way we clearly understand, or at least in a way we understand better than we understand how a creator God could literally exist, either as a physical being or a non-physical one who nevertheless can interact with physical things. Also, despite the fact that there are billions of us, while on the monotheist view there is only one God, each of us is as unique as God is.

What does it mean, though, to say that each of us is unique? Is that just a heart-warming platitude? Is each one of the billions of us unique in any meaningful way? After all, we're told that no two snowflakes are exactly alike, but I doubt if it would bother anyone very long if that turned out to be false. Of course, there is a sense in which even two things that are exactly alike, say two indistinguishable white ping-pong balls, are nevertheless countably unique, but if that is all that we mean when we say that each human being is unique, then what seemed like a heart-warming statement about the value of the individual has turned out to be an uninterestingly elementary fact of applied arithmetic.

But that is not all we mean. When we say that each person in the world is unique, we are talking about the unique perspective from which each of us experiences the world. We can at least partially communicate that to each other. That is why, for example, we can be sure that, even when we can't tell one identical twin from another, they really are two different individuals in a way that goes beyond the mere countably different individuality of a ping-pong ball that is otherwise indistinguishable from another.

That is why the simple answers to the question 'Who am I?', such as stating one's name, or giving an identifying description, or saying, 'I am this person here,' or waving a hand, seem to ignore a deeper meaning to the question, for they seem comparable to identifying a ping-pong ball by saying, for example, that it is the one on the left. In another way, though, they point to the two important differences between a physical object that is a person, such as a human being, and a physical object that isn't, such as a ping-pong ball, namely, that a person has a first-person point of view and can initiate actions. A physical object that is not a person can neither answer the question, 'Who are you?' nor ponder the question, 'Who am I?' And, while some subhuman animals undoubtedly can initiate actions, unlike inanimate objects such as ping-pong balls, they don't have the capacity for reflecting on their own existence over time that is required in order to be able to discover themselves through their actions. Or, if they do, then some non-human animals are persons.

The concept of a *person*, then, is of something that is capable of becoming self-aware and of initiating actions. These two capacities work together. Doing things, in the broad sense that includes thinking, contributes to self-awareness by filling in one's concept of one's self. A human person has the god-like power of creation, not in the sense of literally creating something out of nothing, but in the sense of consciously deciding to make something happen that otherwise would not have happened, so that something then exists that otherwise simply would not have existed.

But this is only part of the answer to the question, 'Who am I?' I am a human person with physical existence, who personifies a particular combination of universally human characteristics, who is self-aware, and who can make things happen that otherwise would not have happened. That much is true of every human person. What makes me me? And what makes me the same person who I was in the past and will be in the future? I've said I have physical existence. We have a perfectly good criterion for identifying a physical object at a particular time and from one time to another: spatio-temporal continuity. A physical object has a location in space at any given time, and from one time to another it traces a continuous path from one spatial location to another. We know how to keep track of physical objects. Of course, we sometimes lose things, but this is a practical problem and not a conceptual one. So, since I have physical existence, one might think this criterion for identifying physical objects is a perfectly good way to answer the questions about my personal identity. What makes me me is that I have the body I have, and no one else does. What makes me the same person who I was in the past and the same one I will be in the future is that the body I have now can be traced back in a continuous path through space-time to the one I had in the past, and it will also be spatio-temporally continuous with the one I will have in the future. However, there is a problem with this answer, not a practical problem as things are, but a conceptual one. The conceptual problem is that I have no difficulty in imagining that I might wake up one morning and find that I have a different body, as happened, for instance, to the fictional protagonist in Franz Kafka's *Metamorphosis*, who found himself one morning with the body of a giant beetle. If the bodily criterion really determines my identity, the preservation of identity, as one body is replaced by another, should be inconceivable. It should be as inconceivable as it would be for an inanimate physical object such as a teapot to have a different body, whether that of another teapot or of something else entirely different like a refrigerator, and yet still to be the same original teapot. But it is not inconceivable for me to have a different body and yet still to be me, as long as I can imagine that I am still conscious or capable of recovering consciousness from a point of view located in that different body.

What is more, it is conceivable that I could still be me without any body at all. In such a case I don't see how I could have any sensory contact with the world, but I could still have a conscious life of thoughts, memories of my previous bodily existence (unless I had never had a body), and dream images. Thus, I could remember interacting with other people, and/or I could dream that I was interacting with other people, but I wouldn't be able really to interact with anyone. Such an existence is undesirable but not inconceivable. I've heard people say, 'The body is just a shell.' This metaphor expresses the truth that a bodily criterion of personal identity is inadequate, but it also expresses a lamentable lack of gratitude for the good that only a body makes possible. And it isn't just the having of any old body or series of bodies that matters to me. I am emotionally attached to this particular body that I have lived with all these years. Still, however, having this particular body isn't what makes me me, since I could conceivably still be me without it.

I've said that I personify a particular combination of universally human characteristics. Is this a way to answer the questions

'What makes me me?' and 'What makes me the same person who I was in the past and will be in the future?' It would be so only if I could be sure that there is a core of unchangeable characteristics that constitute each individual's personality. Actually, I think there probably is such a thing as an unchanging personality that people have. It is exemplified in the kinds of choices a person makes, the kinds of things a person typically likes or dislikes, characteristic things a person worries about or is proud of, etc. However, there are also exceptional cases, usually attributable to disease or some traumatic experience but maybe also due to a religious experience, when a person's personality changes drastically. In such cases, the practical use of the bodily criterion serves to identify who it is who has undergone the personality change. But even if there remains, in every case, an unchanging set of core characteristics, this criterion cannot be the answer to the questions about personal identity. There is another problem, which is that I would also have to be sure that each individual's personality is unique, and I can't be sure of that. For instance, it is easy to imagine that I could have a twin who resembles me exactly not only in his physical appearance, but in his likes and dislikes, temperament, moral character, etc. That which would make us two unique individuals, then, would have to be something other than the facts about us that can be described from a third-person point of view.

I've said that I'm self-aware and that I can make things happen that otherwise would not have happened. What makes me a unique individual, even if somewhere in the universe there is a perfect duplicate of me, is that I'm aware of being me and I'm not aware of being that duplicate. Also, I can make decisions and do things with this body and this personality, but if I had a perfect twin, I would not have the same kind of control over his body and personality. So, then, have I at last found answers to the questions 'What makes me me?' and 'What makes me the same person who I was in the past and will be in the future?' The answer isn't that

I have the body I have, and that no one else does; because I could conceivably have a different one, and somebody else could conceivably have this one. It isn't that I have the particular personality that I do, for my personality could change; and even if it couldn't, it is conceivable someone else could have an exactly similar personality. Is it, then, that I am aware of being me in a way that no one else can be, and that I can do things, like moving my hand right now to write these words, to make something happen that otherwise would not have happened? Well, no. Although I've said something true, I haven't really answered the questions about personal identity.

If I didn't already know who I was, then no objective, third-person description of the persons in a particular room at a particular time, no matter how detailed a description of their bodies and personalities, would tell me whether or not I was one of those persons and, if so, which one. This is an additional, deeper reason why both the bodily and the personality criteria are inadequate. As definitions of personal identity, they are circular. If I say that I = the person with this particular body, or that I = the person with this particular personality, I would have to know already which body or which personality to point to. The same criticism applies even more obviously to the proposed definitions, I = the one and only self of which I am aware in a way in which no one else can be, or I = the one and only self over which I exercise the kind of direct control that no one else can. The concept supposedly being defined appears on both sides of the equals sign.

It is simply an irreducible fact that I am the person who I am, that you are you, that everyone else is whoever he or she is, and that each of us is unique. It can't be explained or analyzed in terms of some more basic fact or set of facts. Is it trivially obvious, then, who I am and what makes me me? No, it isn't, because from the inside I'm still finding out.

One might think, approvingly, that this means that personal

identity is a wonderful mystery that we will never understand. Or, one might think, disapprovingly, that this leaves personal identity as a pointless mystery that we will never understand. A better view than either of those is to think that this means that personal identity is a mystery that hasn't yet been solved but that isn't hopelessly difficult either. The concept of identity is so basic that it can't be defined in any terms that don't presuppose it, but that is not a problem. I can't answer the questions 'What makes me me?' and 'What makes me the same person who I used to be and who I will be?' by applying a definition. But this doesn't mean the questions are meaningless, or that nothing true or important can be said in response to them. Who I am is a mystery that I am solving by living my life.

This is another part of the explanation of what makes life meaningful. It isn't only that, looking ahead to the rest of my life, I will have to live it to see how it turns out, but also that, looking back over the life I have already lived, there is much that remains mysterious, in the good sense of discoveries waiting to be made. Certain memories stand out, and I could recite a broad outline of my autobiography; but I realize that there are vast stretches of the details of daily life that I could remember, if at all, only by a prolonged effort at recollecting and connecting up scattered memories. On the other hand, it is always some precise detail of daily life that is most likely to be vividly remembered in the way that conquers time. The most famous literary example is the reawakening in Marcel Proust's mind of an incident from his childhood, evoked by the taste of a madeleine dipped in tea. When that happens, the experience is not only pleasant, but it also reveals what may be a deep truth: that that earlier moment continued to exist during all the time that it had been forgotten, and that it still will, when it is forgotten once more.

We have already noted a connection between meaningfulness and morality, namely that if life is meaningless there is no point in being moral, and if there are no genuine moral requirements, life is meaningless. Here is another connection. Discovering the answer to the question 'Who am I?' makes life meaningful. Included in that question are the questions 'When did I begin?' and 'When will I end?' The answers to these questions have important implications for some controversial moral issues. We turn to a discussion of these questions in the next chapter.

Chapter 10

The Importance of the Individual (Part II)

When did I begin? When will I end?

He said to them, "Is a lamp brought in to be put under the bushel basket, or under the bed, and not on the lampstand? For there is nothing hidden, except to be disclosed; nor is anything secret, except to come to light. Let anyone with ears to hear listen!"

Mark 4.21-23 (NRSV)

The unanalyzable fact that each of us has a first-person, subjective point of view means that every time a baby is born, it's as if a new world comes into existence, and every time someone dies, it's as if a world has come to an end. Looked at the wrong way, this fact can seem like the ultimate loneliness, but it's also the fountainhead of compassion, and helps explain some of our basic moral intuitions and their connection with the true religion.

No one is in control of the time and circumstances of her or his own birth, and although each of us could choose to control the time and circumstances of her or his death, by committing suicide, most of us - wisely, I think - choose not to do so. In the mean time, one of our most basic moral intuitions is that it is morally wrong to exercise the power each of us has to end someone else's life, unless it is to fulfill some at least equally compelling moral requirement. It is fairly uncontroversial that there are at least some situations where an equally compelling moral requirement exists. For example, it is widely accepted that the prohibition against taking someone else's life is lifted in circumstances of self-defense or when necessary to save the life of some other innocent person. There is controversy, however, over the questions whether or not there are other moral requirements (or prohibitions) that are at least equally compelling as the injunction against taking someone else's life, and, if so, what they are. For example, absolute pacifists believe that defense of one's country in time of war never justifies violating the prohibition against killing people, while others believe that it sometimes does. Among the latter group there are often disagreements over whether or not a particular war is justified. Among those who believe that it is, there can still be disagreements over whether or not particular methods of war are justified. Other examples of controversies involving the prohibition against killing people are disagreements about the morality of the death penalty and about the moral acceptability of euthanasia. What makes these questions serious ones is the underlying recognition that killing someone brings an end to a subjective world every bit as real as one's own.

In Chapter 6 I defended the view that what makes an action moral is that it gives us all a good reason to have less anxiety about meaninglessness, and less fear of suffering, of dying, of going crazy, of being unloved and unlovable; while immoral actions do the opposite. Unless there is compelling justification, the deliberate ending of someone's subjective world gives us all a good reason to feel more anxious about death and meaning-lessness. On the other hand, to refuse to kill under any circum-stances, including those in which killing is required for self-defense or for the defense of one's family, friends, or fellow citizens, also gives us all a good reason to feel more anxious about death, meaninglessness, and being unloved. That is why absolute pacifism is an immoral position.

In that chapter on the connection between morality and religion, I aimed at formulating an objective moral principle that both reinforces and is reinforced by what I take to be the true religion. I wasn't concerned with resolving any particular moral controversy. In fact, I made the point that it is unreasonable to expect religion to resolve moral controversies by itself, since there is always room for disagreement about what the facts are and which circumstances are relevant. Now, having noted the importance of the individual for the true religion, and sensitive to the possible criticism that it is all too easy to utter glittering generalities, I propose in this chapter to apply the general moral principle to three particular moral controversies, namely abortion, embryonic stem cell research, and removing a brain-damaged person from life support. My purpose in doing so is not to show that the true religion can resolve moral controversies all by itself after all, but rather to show how one could apply the objective moral principle implied by the true religion in the light of an examination of relevant empirical facts. These will be case studies, if you will, in applying the principle that moral actions are those that give us all a good reason to have less anxiety about meaninglessness, and less fear of suffering, of dying, of going crazy, of being unloved and unlovable, while immoral actions do the reverse. There are many other interesting and important moral controversies, but these three (abortion, embryonic stem cell research, and removing someone from life support) are particularly interesting because of their connections with the philosophical questions raised at the end of the preceding chapter: When did I begin? When will I end?

From the inside, the self extends to incidents one remembers in the past and to moments one anticipates in the future. I don't have any recollection of coming into consciousness for the very first time. The closest thing to a first-person perspective on what it is like to do so is the religious experience in which everything swirls towards an end and then immediately starts up again, in a sudden intensification of consciousness, as if all the lights have been turned up, as if one has been born again, and everything seems to freshly burst forth, wet and new and seeking attention. Whether or not one has had or remembers such an experience, it doesn't matter that one doesn't remember coming into consciousness for the very first time, since, other than during recurring brief periods of unconsciousness, it seems as if one has always been here. What matters, from a first-person perspective, is being conscious, recovering consciousness whenever one loses it, and the quality of that consciousness in terms of joy or misery. Hoping for immortality would be hoping that things go on like this forever. Accepting mortality is accepting that there will come a time when one will lose consciousness and never regain it.

Each of us also has a unique human body. As I've argued, that body is not what makes a person whoever he or she is, because it is conceivable that he or she could have a different body or none at all. However, just because something is conceivable is not a good reason to think it has ever happened or ever will. There is abundant empirical evidence in support of the view that the life of that body is a necessary condition for being conscious and having a first-person perspective on the world:

- The body is always there whenever one checks.
- We don't know of any human person who doesn't have a body.
- There has never been a time when one undoubtedly existed and yet one's body did not.
- Scientists have established correlations between reports of particular subjective experiences and neural activity in particular areas of the brain.

Because I have this body, I extend my sense of self to times and places it has occupied and will occupy (as long as I'm alive), whether or not I remember or can anticipate being conscious then and there. For example, I have no identifiable memories of being an infant, but I don't conclude that I didn't come into existence until about three years after this body of mine was born. (I think I was three at one of the earliest times I can remember.) Neither do I conclude that I temporarily ceased to exist during periods when

I was asleep with no memories of any dreams, and that I then popped back into existence upon awakening. Nor do I think I ceased to exist while unconscious during surgery.

We all know what it is like to fall asleep and what it is like to wake up. Many of us also know what it is like to be rendered unconscious by an anesthesiologist and what it is like to regain consciousness afterwards. (The latter pair are something like irresistibly swiftly falling into a deep, dark hole and then re-emerging with the sensation that no time has passed.) But since there is good reason not to equate existing as a person with being conscious, namely the fact that we are not always conscious, this knowledge does not tell us what it is like to begin to exist or to cease to exist. It is most reasonable to believe that each of us came into existence before becoming conscious, just as we can continue to exist while unconscious, and it is most likely that we will lose consciousness before ceasing to exist at death. Therefore, we don't have any special inside view, or first-person perspective, on what it is like to begin to exist or to cease existing.

A possible objection to that conclusion would be to point out that we have all heard of the first-person reports of those who have been pronounced dead but who have then recovered. They tell of being blissfully drawn in by a warm, bright light but then being pulled back by the realization that it was not yet time, that they had more to do in this world. I see no reason to doubt such reports. However, the implication is usually taken to be that there is a kind of conscious existence after death rather than that people who have had such an experience know what it is like to be on the verge of ceasing to exist. At any rate, there isn't any way in which the question can be resolved from a first-person perspective, unless we find out when we die, and stay dead, that we continue to be conscious, somehow, after death. Either way, we're never going to succeed in knowing what it's like to cease to exist, although we might find out what it's like to be about to cease to exist, since either we never cease to exist or else we do go out of existence but simultaneously lose the ability to know what anything is like. So the conclusion stands: we don't have a first-person perspective on what it is like to cease to exist any more than we do on what it is like to begin to exist. Therefore, we drop the questions about what it is like from a subjective point of view and turn to the questions: What is it, objectively, for a unique human individual to come into existence? What is it, objectively, for one to cease to exist?

We conventionally mark the beginning of a person's life with the date of his or her birth, and the end with the date of death. This is more than mere convention, though, since birth and death are clearly observable events. However, birth is certainly not the springing into existence out of nothingness of the human organism. As for death, the use of life-saving technologies like respirators and feeding tubes has produced problematic cases that raise the question whether a person who is permanently unconscious is, in any real sense, still alive.

Let us first look at the question of when the life of a unique human being comes into existence and then return later to the question of when such an existence comes to an end.

When did I begin?

In Chapter 6, I wrote that a woman with an unwanted pregnancy contemplating the moral permissibility of abortion should ask herself the question whether having the abortion would give us all a good reason to have less anxiety about meaninglessness and less fear of suffering, of dying, of being unloved and unlovable. If it would, then it would be the morally right thing to do. If, instead, it would give us all a good reason to have more of such anxiety and fear, then it would be morally wrong. If it did neither, that is, if upon reflection we would have no good reason to feel either less or more anxiety and fear as a result of her decision to terminate her pregnancy; then it would be morally permissible. Clearly, whether or not we have such a reason depends on the answer to

The Importance of the Individual (Part II)

the question: What is it for a unique human individual to come into existence? If the answer is that a unique human individual comes into existence at birth and not before, then abortion would be much more likely to be morally permissible or even morally praiseworthy, depending on the circumstances, than if a unique human individual comes into existence at the moment of conception. Of course, the answer might be that an individual comes into existence neither at birth nor at conception, but rather at some time in between. Actually, as I shall try to explain, we have good reason to think that it is at a time in between, but at a time much closer to conception than to birth, namely, at fourteen days after conception.[60]

For each of us, there was a particular sperm that fertilized a particular egg in a process that resulted, ultimately, in his or her birth and in the existence of the person who is either writing (in my case) or reading this (in yours). If either that egg or that sperm had been destroyed before they fused, the individual in question would never have come into existence. Short of destruction, if, for whatever reason, the two had never fused - if, say, that sperm had fused with a different egg instead or with none at all, or if that egg had fused with a different sperm or with none at all - then, again, the individual in question would never have come into existence. We know that a vast majority of human ova never do fuse with a sperm, and an even vaster majority of human sperm never fuse with an ovum. Contemplating these facts can give one an uncanny sense of the contingency of one's own existence which might contribute to existential anxiety, although I confess that in my own case this does it much less so than does just the bare fact of my dependency on the present continued good health and safety of my body. Maybe, ironically, that is because the latter are at least partially under my control. Anyway, for the most part any existential anxiety provoked by the improbability of one's coming into existence in the first place won't be due to any action subject to moral judgment, since whether or not a particular egg fuses with a particular sperm is mostly not subject to anyone's control. True, we know how to take measures to prevent conception from taking place, ranging from abstaining from copulation to use of pills, condoms and other mechanical or chemical means. However, while the choice to avoid conception is subject to moral judgment and could be morally unacceptable if made for foolishly selfish reasons, it wouldn't be morally unacceptable on the grounds that it kills a unique human individual. Even if it involves the destruction of sperm or egg, it wouldn't be the killing of an individual human, since a sperm or an egg is not a unique human individual. There is clearly a valid moral distinction between choosing to act in a way that merely prevents someone or other from coming into existence and choosing to act in a way that results in the death of someone who already exists. Otherwise, the only innocent ones would be those who choose to forgo any means of birth control while having as much promiscuous sex as physically possible.

There are some methods of birth control that don't work by preventing the fusion of sperm and egg but instead prevent a fertilized egg from attaching to the lining of the uterus and developing a placenta. Does this cross the line so that it does constitute the destruction of a unique human individual? Let's review some facts about human embryology. A human zygote is a single cell created by the fusion of egg and sperm, with the full complement of 46 chromosomes necessary for the development of a human individual. Within hours the cell divides, each of the daughter cells divides, each of the resulting cells in turn divides, and so on, until a blastocyst is formed. This is a hollow ball of cells, each one of which is a totipotent stem cell. That is, each one of those cells is not yet differentiated into a cell of a particular kind of tissue or organ, and it is capable of developing into a cell of any kind of tissue or organ. At fourteen days after conception, some of the cells begin to specialize, and the "primitive streak" appears. This is the precursor of the spinal cord and central nervous system.

From this point on, the cells begin to be irreversibly specialized into types that will perform different functions. Some of them will develop into the placenta, and the rest will form the different tissues and organs of the developing embryo.

Because of these biological facts, it is reasonable to believe that a unique human individual comes into existence at fourteen days after conception, when the cells begin to be dedicated to special functions, and the primitive streak appears. Why not before? Why not at the moment when the sperm and egg fuse, forming the zygote? We can see why there is not yet a unique human individual before conception, since each gamete (ovum or sperm) has only half the chromosomes needed to form the genetic identity of a human being, and we know that if either of them had fused with a different partner instead, then a different genetic identity would have been determined. But once egg and sperm have fused, those alternate possibilities are closed off, so this would seem to be the point in time to which one could trace back one's identity as a unique human individual, the earliest moment of one's existence. However, there is good reason to think that it isn't. The reason is that one's genetic identity, which is determined by the fusion of a particular egg with a particular sperm, is not sufficient to determine one's identity as a unique human individual. If it were, then identical (monozygotic) twins would not be two unique individuals but would be one unique individual inhabiting two separate bodies. What, then, is sufficient to determine one's identity as a unique human individual? At this stage of human life, it is the biological process of cell differentiation that closes off the possibility of the embryo splitting into two genetically identical ones. This occurs by the fourteenth day after conception, when the primitive streak appears. By that time, the zygote or very early embryo would have either split or not.

I say "at this stage of human life" because later, when one has become consciously self-aware, with a first-person perspective, that perspective is sufficient to determine one's identity as a unique human individual. Suppose, for example, it were possible for an adult to split into two copies, as it is for a zygote or very early embryo (within the first few days after conception). Then, even if both resulting people were genetically identical and psychologically continuous with the original person who split, there would still be a fact as to which one of the two, if either one, is the same unique human individual as the original person. From the first-person perspective of that original person, he or she would be looking out of the eyes of one of the resulting people and not the other, or else he or she would have lost consciousness permanently and the resulting people each would have just come into existence. In contrast, since a zygote or very early embryo doesn't have a first-person perspective, there is no fact as to which twin, if any, it would be if it split. Rather, there simply is not yet a uniquely determined individual until there is enough cell specialization to render viable splitting biologically impossible.

I don't expect the reader to be convinced quite yet that this is the right view, so I'll say more. Suppose you had a twin, and you were to ask yourself, 'When did I come into existence as a unique individual human being?' The answer that would make the most sense would be that it was when the early embryo, that was the biological origin of both you and your twin, split in two. If you answer, instead, that it was when the zygote, that was the biological origin of both you and your twin, came into existence, then the implication would be that in those early hours or days before the split you were fused with your twin and yet you still somehow existed already as a unique individual. But there would be nothing about that zygote or early embryo at any time before it split that would identify one part of it as you and the other part as your twin.

'But I'm not a twin,' you might reply (unless you are one), 'so why should the mere possibility that I might have been one give me any reason to think that in my case I didn't come into existence until the time when the embryo out of which I developed had enough cell specialization to make it biologically impossible for part of me to split off and twin into a genetically identical copy?'

Well, consider the particular egg and the particular sperm to which you can trace your biological origin. A good reason, to think that you didn't come into existence until that egg and that sperm fused, is that each of them might have fused with a different partner or with none at all. But after all, just as it is a mere possibility that you might have had a twin, so also it is a mere possibility that that egg and that sperm might have fused with a different partner instead or with none at all. In fact, they did fuse with each other. You want to dismiss as unimportant the possibility that you might have had a twin. You want to say that maybe a twin doesn't come into existence as a unique individual until the zygote or very early embryo splits but that we non-twins came into existence as unique individuals at the moment of conception. But you would have just as good a reason, or, more precisely, no better a reason, to dismiss the possibility that the particular egg and the particular sperm, that in fact are your biological origin, might not have fused with each other. So, you would have just as good a reason (no better a reason) to say, 'That mere possibility doesn't matter. In fact, they did fuse. So, I already existed as a unique individual even before conception. I consisted of two spatially separated parts of unequal size and of different origin.' But then when did you come into existence? It can't be the moment when that sperm and that egg first came into existence, since it is highly improbable that they came into existence at the same moment. Should you say, then, that it was when the first of the two came into existence, that, say, you were an ovum until the sperm that was later to join with that ovum came into existence, at which point you were both that ovum and that sperm and that you existed in two separate locations until the later time at which they fused? Or, should you say that you didn't exist until the second of the two came into existence? There is no reason to choose one of these alternatives rather than the other. It makes much more sense not to dismiss as "mere" the possibility that each of those gametes just as easily might have fused with a different partner or, as is, after all, much more likely, that it might have failed to fuse with any. Because of this possibility, it's much more plausible that you didn't exist before the zygote out of which you grew had come into existence, thus closing off the alternate possibilities of non-fusion and of fusion with other partners. Similarly, because of the biological possibility that that zygote could have individuated into twins rather than into a single individual, it is more plausible that you didn't come into existence until enough cell divisions and cell specializations occurred so that it was no longer possible for the very early embryo to split into two.

What follows from this is that there is an important moral dividing line between intentionally doing something that one knows will result in the destruction of a zygote or a blastocyst and intentionally doing something that one knows will result in the destruction of an embryo with cells that have already begun to specialize. The former is morally equivalent to using birth control, abstaining from copulation, etc., i.e., knowingly doing something that will prevent any number of people who don't yet exist from coming into existence. The latter is morally equivalent to killing someone who already exists. It follows that "morning-after" birth control, very early abortion (within 14 days of conception), and embryonic stem cell research (which destroys embryos within the first few days after their creation) are all morally permissible or praiseworthy, depending on the circumstances; while all but very early abortions are morally wrong, except in cases where there is compelling justification, such as when continued pregnancy would be a threat to the life of the mother.

A significant difference between abortion and murder is that murder, but not abortion, gives us all a good reason to have more fear of dying prematurely. If there are murderers about, the life of each of us is at more risk than if no one ever commits murder. Abortion doesn't in the same way threaten any of us who already have been born with an increased risk of premature death. Instead, it threatens the lives of those who already exist but who haven't yet been born, although they don't know it. So, it doesn't inspire the same fear of one's own premature death. However, it gives us all a good reason to have more anxiety about meaninglessness, because it shows a disregard for the value of the life of an individual.

Because of this difference between abortion and murder, and because it is not as obvious that an abortion, unless it is very early, kills someone who already exists as it is that murder does so, the degree of the immorality of abortion, when it is immoral, is likely to be less than that of the immorality of murder. However, the degree of immorality of abortion is going to be closer to that of murder than it is to that of theft, vandalism, or fraud, because the unjustified taking of life gives us all more good reason to be anxious than does the unjustified taking or destruction of property.

When will I end?

As I've said, what matters from a first-person perspective is that I am conscious now and that I hope to continue to be conscious or to recover consciousness whenever I lose it. This explains a difference between the moral concern about the beginning of a person's existence and the concern about the end of a person's existence. Even though a person is not conscious until months after he or she has come into existence, killing him or her before that time makes it impossible for him or her ever to achieve the great good of becoming conscious and self-aware. In contrast, if one contemplates a possible situation in the future, near the end of life, in which one has already enjoyed that good before lapsing into permanent unconsciousness, there is no reason for one to want to be kept alive with a respirator or a feeding tube. Being alive and remaining so is a necessary condition for being conscious and recovering consciousness whenever one loses it, but it isn't sufficient. That it is necessary is why it is important that one not be killed before ever coming to consciousness for the first time or at any time before one has lost consciousness for the last time. That it is not sufficient is why it can be unimportant, and even undesirable, to remain alive when another necessary condition for consciousness, a brain healthy enough to cause it, is lacking. If there is hope that the brain can recover enough so that it can cause one to become conscious again, then it is important that one be kept alive to keep open that possibility. But if it is clear that there is no reason to hope the brain can recover enough to cause consciousness, then there is no reason to want to be kept alive.

Some would say that a person who has become permanently unconscious is already dead. We have the expression "brain dead" and definitions of what it is to be "clinically dead." But doubts are raised by those aforementioned reports of people who have been pronounced clinically dead and who lived to tell the tale. Perhaps a better approach is to accept the classical conception of death, i.e., the permanent cessation of circulation and respiration. Since we know that it is possible to resuscitate someone within a certain limited period of time, we are obligated to try to do so, when these vital signs have only recently ceased. But before long, if those efforts fail, we have no doubt that the person is dead. It's quite normal for a person to become permanently unconscious before his or her last heartbeat and last breath. It's just that we now have technology that enables us in some cases to extend indefinitely that gap in time between final loss of consciousness and final loss of life. Such technology is useful when there is hope that the person might eventually recover consciousness, but it's a nuisance otherwise. Hard cases arise when there is less than overwhelming scientific evidence as to whether the person is conscious or might recover consciousness. This is complicated by the fact that the person making the decision is not usually an expert in the field and has to decide who really is an expert, and which expert to trust if there are several of them and they disagree. A further complication is that there may be two or more people who are morally responsible for making the decision and they might not agree. The crucial question in such a situation is whether it is rational to hope that the person might recover consciousness. Sometimes the answer to that question is not at all clear, but there are also many cases in which it is quite clear that there is no medically sound reason to hope that the person could ever regain consciousness.

Some people think it is always rational to hope. They reason as follows: God can do anything that is logically possible. So, even if our best medical science tells us that there is no hope that a person with extensive brain damage could recover consciousness, there still is hope. There always is, because God could make it happen.

What is symbolized by this view of God as a miracle worker who can intervene to save people in hopeless situations? It symbolizes the limits of human knowledge. The fact that there are important things outside our control is, on the intellectual side, the fact that our knowledge is limited. Scientific knowledge is, in a fundamental way, never the final word. Even the most well confirmed scientific hypothesis is always open to refutation by further evidence. However, this is no reason to keep someone alive using a respirator or a feeding tube, if our best medical evidence tells us there is no hope that he or she will ever recover consciousness. To hope for a miracle is to hope that something will happen to refute our best scientific understanding. But that is just as likely to happen if we turn off the respirator or remove the feeding tube as it is if we don't.

Suppose there is overwhelming scientific evidence that someone who has lost consciousness has such severe brain damage that she or he will never recover consciousness. It isn't irrational to hope, nevertheless, that by some miracle her or his brain will be restored and that she or he will regain consciousness. But it would be irrational to base a decision on whether or not to remove this person from life support on such a hope for a miracle. That would just be a pretense of understanding what one does not understand: whether, and if so, how, some action of one's own can have any effect on the occurrence of a miracle.

Still, it is all too easy to be misinformed or to make a mistake in reasoning, as is clear when it comes to our own mistakes when we are aware of them. So, we shouldn't condemn too harshly someone who confuses religious hope with scientifically justified hope if the only harm done is that someone who is permanently unconscious is kept alive longer than he or she would have wanted. Rather, we should attempt to explain why it is harmful. The reason it is undesirable to be kept alive after one has become permanently unconscious is that one is then completely passive, dependent, and pitiful, so that one's life will have appended to it a period of meaningless existence. The reason it wouldn't be a great harm is that one would be totally unaware of it, and the period of meaningless existence wouldn't take anything away from the meaningfulness of one's life before one lapsed into permanent unconsciousness.

It may well be that I have made mistakes in my reasoning to the conclusions 1) that all but very early abortions require compelling moral justification, while embryonic stem-cell research doesn't, and 2) that hoping for a miracle does not justify keeping someone alive on life support. If so, I should be indebted to anyone who can explain those mistakes. I am quite convinced that it can be difficult to know what is the right thing to do, which is why there are moral controversies such as the one about the morality of abortion, of embryonic stem cell research, and of taking someone off life support. And it can be difficult to distinguish between religious hope and scientifically justified hope. The true religious view is that we should hope that, by persevering, we will be able to tell the difference and to repent of any moral mistakes we come to recognize.

Epilogue

> They shall be turned back and utterly put to shame — those
> who trust in carved images, who say to cast images, "You are
> our gods."
>
> Isaiah 42.17 (NRSV)

In order to further clarify the claims I've made about the true
religion, let's review some main points and consider some
possible objections.

God is a symbol of something true, namely that there are things
that really matter to each of us but that escape our individual and
collective control, such as whether or not we ever suffer, whether
or not we ever die, whether or not we are loved, whether or not
everything is fundamentally all right.

A possible objection is that this is to make God a fiction, to
deny that God exists. It is like saying that Santa Claus is a myth
we have created to symbolize the fact that we give gifts to our
children at Christmas.

The answer to the objection is that there is a great difference
between what God symbolizes and what Santa Claus symbolizes.
Our practice of gift giving at Christmas is something that we
control, either individually or collectively. It is outside one's
control as an individual whether or not the culture in which one
was brought up practices gift giving at Christmas; but if one is
willing to defy social pressure, one could decide not to participate; and if enough individuals did that, the practice would die
out. Then, through the collective actions of enough individuals, a
new custom might arise to replace it. In contrast, nothing we can
do, individually or collectively, is ever going to result in our being
in control of everything that matters. So, that which we symbolize
or try to name by talking about God is not a creation of ours. It is

not under our control. It is that which will forever elude our control. We may invent fictions about it, but those fictions are not it. The Jewish prohibition against uttering the name of God and the saying, that the Tao that can be named is not the Tao, are consistent with this. God is more than a literary creation. The work of a great writer or of any great artist is god-like in a high degree. The day-to-day actions of each of us are similarly god-like in that we thereby create something that otherwise wouldn't have existed. But unlike any fictional character, God is what escapes the control of even the greatest literary artist. By the way, I suspect that the greatest masterpieces of art, though they seem perfect to us, were known by the artists who created them to be flawed. Nevertheless, a great artist justifiably takes pride in having created something beautiful that otherwise would not have existed. Likewise, each of us should be proud of every small act of decency we do, well aware of our shortcomings.

Another possible objection is that we don't need to indulge in this childish or primitive personification. What eludes our control and thwarts our ambitions, but also makes possible our joys as well as our sorrows, consists of two classes of things: 1) the natural laws of the impersonal, physical universe, and 2) the actions of other people. To create a personalized symbol (or symbols) for impersonal natural laws is to distort the truth. And we don't need to create a personalized symbol for what is already personal: the ways in which we are affected by the actions of other people.

I am sympathetic to this objection. It pinpoints what is false about false religion: 1) the idolatry of clinging to a fake under-standing of nature via supernatural explanations, and 2) the idolatry of worshipping a symbolic personification while neglecting real people. The answer to the objection is that the God of the true religion symbolizes, not a pretense of understanding what we don't understand, but rather the limits of our under-standing. And He doesn't symbolize a super person who wants to be worshipped. That is an aspect of the symbol, not the reality that is being symbolized, which is the tenderness we feel towards ourselves and each other when we are aware of our common mortality and vulnerability to anxiety and suffering, as well as the deep contentment and joy that comes from being alive, conscious, awake, aware, and active.

Salvation is the realization that despite or because of the fact that there are important things outside our control, everything is fundamentally all right.

In an earlier chapter I've already dealt with the objections: 1) that this is just a philosophy of life and not a religious view, and 2) that everything is not fundamentally all right because people suffer and do evil things. Another possible objection I haven't yet answered is that there is no way we can really know whether or not everything is fundamentally all right, so no one can credibly claim to have had such a realization. This objection is reinforced by the fact that I've said that faith is living up to this realization and sin is not living up to it, because then I can't say that the realization itself is a matter of faith. The answer to this objection is that it is just as audacious to claim to know that no one can really know whether everything is fundamentally all right as it is to claim to know that everything is fundamentally all right. Admittedly, this is a *tu quoque*. It only shows that the critic is not on firmer ground. It doesn't show that the claim being defended is on firm ground. I can only say that I think I do know that everything is fundamentally all right, but I've admitted that this is just a verbal formula for expressing something that is as much an emotional response as it is an intellectual conviction, and that the depth or intensity of it wavers, a fact that is aptly symbolized as the alternation between fear of God and trust in God.

Religion differs radically from both science and politics. Science aims at the kind of understanding that gives us more predictive power and control, while the goal of politics is to attain more control by acting together with others, where the means includes threat of force collectively supported. In contrast, the essence of religion is an individual confronting the fact that there are important things over which he or she cannot gain control either scientifically or politically or in any other way.

A possible objection is that the religions we know by name: Judaism, Christianity, Islam, Hinduism, Buddhism, etc., are social systems that include rituals and a distinction between sacred and profane or holy and unholy, and that, in fact, do succeed in having political influence. An individual, confronting his or her own existential anxiety about meaninglessness, fear of suffering and death, of being unloved and unlovable, might be called "spiritual"; but when we say that someone is religious, we mean to identify her or him as a member of a named religion.

The answer to this objection is that such a sociological view of religion misses the point of religion, which necessarily involves a distinction between true religion and false religion. True religion is individualistic because the social structures that we create collectively cannot change the fact that there are things that we care about that are beyond our control.

Does it follow that someone who follows the true religion should refuse to participate in the rituals of any named religion? I don't think so. I've tried to explain how in my view the true religion is consistent with "true Christianity," and I suspect someone raised in a different religious tradition might similarly understand a true version of that tradition to symbolize the true religion. This isn't to adopt a relativistic view of the truth about religion, though, because what is being symbolized in various ways would have to be one and the same fundamental truth, which I have tried to express by saying that there are important things outside our control, and that everything, including that fact, is fundamentally all right. If I am wrong about that, then I am wrong about religion. There is, in religion, something to be right or wrong about.

Death can't wipe out the objective meaningfulness of subjective experiences that have already happened.

A possible objection is that this is trivially true. Of course death can't make it as if something that has happened hasn't happened; nothing can. But so what? What we dread about death is the cutting off of any further experience, not the logically impossible trick of making it true that something that has already happened never happened.

The answer to this objection is that just because one can intellectually grasp a logical fact quite easily, it doesn't necessarily follow that it is of little importance. One can still be in the grip of an instinctual fear that what one intellectually realizes can't happen, can happen after all. No one can die my death for me, so it can seem overwhelmingly important that death will bring my subjective awareness to an end and so it can seem not to matter that death can't erase the fact that I've lived exactly the life that I've lived. Looking forward to the point of view I will have or rather fail to have when I'm dead, it will be as if nothing has happened, is happening, or ever will happen, because I'll be dead. To counter this way of thinking, it is important, and not at all trivial, to remind oneself, that from one's point of view, now, looking forward to a future in which one will be dead, one's future lack of subjective awareness is not all that matters. The objective reality that one now knows to exist, through the medium of one's subjective awareness, also matters. It matters how things are, whether or not one knows how they are. Otherwise, it wouldn't matter whether one's beliefs are true or false. So it matters, for example, whether or not people I love will go on living after I'm dead, and whether or not their joys will outweigh their suffering, even though I won't be aware of it. Likewise, it matters that my death won't erase the life I've already lived.

There is a subjective experience that supports the realization of this logical fact. I've mentioned it before. It is the experience, I believe we all have now and then, of momentarily reliving vividly a sensory experience from the past. The freshness of a morning, for instance, is exactly the same that one has felt before in just the same way. Far from inferring that that earlier time would have been lost forever if one hadn't recalled it just now, one has the conviction that it had gone on existing all along and always will.

Notes

1. Santayana, George. New York: Dover Publications, 1955, p. 104, footnote 1.
2. *Vatican Sayings*, 61, in Epicurus. *The Essential Epicurus: Letters, Principal Doctrines, Vatican Sayings, and Fragments*, translated by Eugene O'Connor. Amherst, New York: Prometheus Books, 1993, p. 83.
3. Marx, K. and Engels, F. 'Introduction to a Critique of Hegelian Philosophy of Right,' in *Collected Works*. London: Lawrence & Wishart, 1975.
4. Epicurus, p. 62, *Letter to Menoeceus*, 123 and p. 69, *Principal Doctrines*, 1.
5. Epicurus, p. 79, *Vatican Sayings*, 31.
6. Epicurus, p. 67, *Letter to Menoeceus*, 134.
7. Epicurus, p. 63, *Letter to Menoeceus*, 125.
8. Epicurus, p. 72, *Principal Doctrines*, 20.
9. Epicurus, p. 81, *Vatican Sayings*, 47.
10. Epicurus, p. 82, *Vatican Sayings*, 48.
11. Frankl, Viktor E. *Man's Search for Meaning*. New York: Washington Square Press, 1984, p. 104.
12. Tillich, Paul. *The Courage to Be*, 2nd edition. New Haven and London: Yale University Press, 2000, p. 176.
13. Robinson, James M., ed., *The Nag Hammadi Library in English*. San Francisco: HarperCollins, 1990, p. 138.
14. The texts of these historic church documents are published online at the website of the Center for Reformed Theology and Apologetics, http://www.reformed.org/documents/index.html.
15. Miles, Jack. *God: A Biography*. New York: Vintage Books, 1995.
16. Miles, p. 187.
17. Many materialists deny that they deny that we have conscious experiences. For an argument to the conclusion that they do

deny it, see Searle, John R. *The Mystery of Consciousness*. New York: *The New York Review of Books*, 1997, pp. 97-131.
18. Searle, John R. *Mind: A Brief Introduction*. New York and Oxford: Oxford University Press, 2004, pp. 80-83.
19. Locke, John. *A Letter Concerning Toleration*. Amherst, New York: Prometheus Books, 1990, pp. 40-41.
20. Saint Augustine, *Enchiridion*, trans. J.F. Shaw, from *The Works of Aurelius Augustine*, vol. IX, Rev. Marcus Dods, ed., Edinburgh: T. & T. Clark, 1892, Chs. XI-XII. The relevant excerpt is reprinted in Denise, Theodore C; White, Nicholas P. and Peterfreund, Sheldon, P. *Great Traditions in Ethics*, 12th ed. Belmont, California: Thomson Higher Education, 2008, pp. 62-3.
21. Dawkins, Richard. *River Out of Eden*. New York: HarperCollins, 1995, p. 132-133.
22. Stephen Hawking speculates that when a quantum theory of gravity is developed it might turn out that there is no Big Bang singularity: 'In the classical theory of gravity,…there are only two possible ways the universe can behave: either it has existed for an infinite time, or else it had a beginning at a singularity at some finite time in the past. In the quantum theory of gravity, on the other hand, a third possibility arises…. [I]t is possible for space-time to be finite in extent and yet to have no singularities that formed a boundary or edge. Space-time would be like the surface of the earth, only with two more dimensions. The surface of the earth is finite in extent but it doesn't have a boundary or edge.' Then it would follow that 'there would be no singularities at which the laws of science broke down and no edge of space-time at which one would have to appeal to God or some new law to set the boundary conditions for space-time. One could say, "the boundary condition of the universe is that it has no boundary." The universe would be completely self-contained and not affected by anything outside itself. It would neither

be created nor destroyed. It would just BE.' *A Brief of History of Time*. New York: Bantam Books, 1990, pp. 135-136.

23. See, for instance, Lewis, C.S. *Mere Christianity*. San Francisco: HarperCollins, 2001.

24. Jung, C. G. *Synchronicity: An Acausal Connecting Principle*. Princeton: Princeton University Press, 1973.

25. Jung, p. 8.

26. Jung, pp. 109-110.

27. Searle, John R. *Mind, Language and Society*. New York: Basic Books, 1999, p. 107.

28. Epicurus, p. 69. *Principal Doctrines*, 2.

29. Epicurus, p. 69. *Principal Doctrines*, 4.

30. Epicurus, p. 73. *Principal Doctrines*, 27.

31. Epicurus, p. 97. *Fragments*, 54.

32. Epicurus, p. 80. *Vatican Sayings*, 38.

33. This is not a typo. It is the adjectival form of "scientism."

34. For extensive argumentation along this line, see *Luther: De Servo Arbitrio*, in Rupp, E.G. and Watson, P.S., translators and editors, *Luther and Erasmus: Free Will and Salvation*. Philadelphia: The Westminster Press, 1969, pp. 239-246.

35. For such a view, see Dennett, D.C., *Freedom Evolves*. New York: Penguin Books, 2003.

36. This objection is a modern version of one that the Schoolmen expressed as a distinction between the necessity of the consequence and the necessity of the consequent. Luther, in his defense of the view that our having free will is incompatible with God's immutable will, effectively showed why this distinction was irrelevant. (See Luther and Erasmus, pp. 119-21 and 239-49.) For the modern version, see Prof. Norman Swartz's presentation in the article 'Foreknowledge and Free Will' in the *Internet Encyclopedia of Philosophy*, at http://www.iep.utm.edu/f/foreknow.htm and his paper '"The" Modal Fallacy' at http://www.sfu.ca/philosophy/swartz/modal_fallacy.htm.

37. For a good account, see Herrick, Paul. *The Many Worlds of Logic.* Fort Worth: Harcourt Brace, 2000, pp. 505-508.

38. For an argument along these lines, see Westphal, Jonathan. 'A new way with the Consequence Argument and the fixity of the laws.' *Analysis* 63: 208-212, July 2003.

39. Popper, Karl R. 'On the Status of Science and Metaphysics,' in *Conjectures and Refutations: The Growth of Scientific Knowledge.* London: Routledge, 1989, pp. 193-200.

40. Kane, Robert. *The Significance of Free Will.* Oxford: Oxford University Press, 1966, pp. 126-139.

41. I owe this example to Steven M. Cahn. See Cahn, Steven. M. 'Random Choices' in *Puzzles and Perplexities.* Lanham, Maryland: Rowman and Littlefield, 2002, pp. 15-17. Incidentally, another example of synchronicity is that one evening after I had been working on this chapter and had used Cahn's example, I was watching a TV medical drama, and there occurred a scene which featured a sick magician who frequently fanned out a deck of cards and asked the attendant doctors, who were having difficulty in diagnosing his illness, to 'pick a card, any card,' and who, of course, unerringly and spectacularly identified the card that had been selected.

42. James, William. 'The Dilemma of Determinism,' An address to the Harvard Divinity Students published in the *Unitarian Review,* 1884. Also available in *James: Essays on Faith and Morals,* Longmans, Green and Co., 1949, and in Kolak, Daniel and Martin, Raymond, *The Experience of Philosophy,* Belmont, California: Wadsworth/Thomson Learning, 5th ed., 2002, pp. 194-201.

43. Kierkegaard, Soren. *Fear and Trembling,* trans. A. Hannay. London: Penguin Books, 2003, pp. 145-146.

44. Epicurus, Letter to Menoeceus, 132, p. 66.

45. Epicurus, Principal Doctrines, 40, p. 76; Vatican Sayings, 15, 23, 34, 39, pp. 78-80; 52, 56, p. 82.

46. Epicurus, Principal Doctrines, 17, p. 71; 31-38, pp. 74-75.
47. See the quotation from the Athanasian Creed in Chapter 3.
48. Luther and Erasmus, pp. 174-175.
49. Luther and Erasmus, p. 213.
50. Luther and Erasmus, p. 214.
51. Luther and Erasmus, p. 41.
52. Luther and Erasmus, p. 212.
53. If this is easier for you to imagine in the case of life-threatening illness than in the case of a psychedelic experience, I recommend the account of the world's first intentional LSD trip by Albert Hoffman, the Swiss chemist who discovered LSD, in Hoffman, Albert. *LSD: My Problem Child*, trans. J. Ott. Sarasota, Florida: Multidisciplinary Association for Psychedelic Studies, 2005.
54. For this view of Christianity, see Schweitzer, Albert. *The Quest of the Historical Jesus*, trans. W. Montgomery. Mineola, New York: Dover Publications, Inc., 2005, especially Chap. XIX, 'Thoroughgoing Scepticism and Thoroughgoing Eschatology.'
55. Kierkegaard, pp. 60-61.
56. For an interpretation consistent with this view, according to which Abraham was calling God's bluff, see Jack Miles's biography of God, pp. 58-61.
57. Schweitzer, p. 390.
58. Published on the World Wide Web at anychristianlyrics.com.
59. Published on the World Wide Web at oldielyrics.com.
60. For an excellent, thorough exposition of this position, see Ford, Norman M. *When did I begin?* Cambridge: Cambridge University Press, 1991.

Bibliography

Antony, Louise M. *Philosophers Without Gods: Meditations on Atheism and the Secular Life*. New York: Oxford University Press, 2007.

Behe, Michael J. *Darwin's Black Box: The Biochemical Challenge to Evolution*. New York: The Free Press, 2003.

Bloom, Harold. *Jesus and Yahweh: The Names Divine*. New York: Riverhead Books, 2007.

Cahn, Steven. M. 'Random Choices' in *Puzzles and Perplexities*. Lanham, Maryland: Rowman and Littlefield, 2002.

Chesterton, G. K. *Orthodoxy*. Mineola, New York: Dover Publications, 2004.

Coogan, Michael D., ed.; Brettler, Marc Z., Newsom, Carol A., Perkins, Pheme, assoc. eds. *The New Oxford Annotated Bible*, 3rd ed. Oxford: Oxford University Press, 2001.

Dawkins, Richard. *The Blind Watchmaker: Why the evidence of evolution reveals a universe without design*. New York: W.W. Norton, 1996.

————————. *River Out of Eden*. New York: HarperCollins, 1995.

Dembski, William A. *Intelligent Design: The Bridge Between Science & Theology*. Downers Grove, Illinois: InterVarsity Press, 1999.

Denise, Theodore C., White, Nicholas P. and Peterfreund, Sheldon P. *Great Traditions in Ethics*, 12th ed. Belmont, California: Thomson Higher Education, 2008.

Dennett, Daniel C. *Breaking the Spell: Religion as a Natural Phenomenon*. New York: Penguin Books, 2007.

Dennett, Daniel C. *Freedom Evolves*. New York: Penguin Books, 2003.

Durkheim, Emile. *The Elementary Forms of Religious Life*, translated by Carol Cosman. Oxford: Oxford University Press, 2001.

Edwards, Jonathan, and others. *Sinners in the Hands of an Angry*

God, and other Puritan Sermons. Mineola, New York: Dover Publications, 2005.

Ehrman, Bart D. *God's Problem: How the Bible Fails to Answer Our Most Important Question – Why We Suffer.* New York: HarperOne, 2008.

Epicurus. *The Essential Epicurus: Letters, Principal Doctrines, Vatican Sayings, and Fragments,* translated by Eugene O'Connor. Amherst, New York: Prometheus Books, 1993.

Flew, Antony, with Varghese, Roy Abraham. *There Is A God: How the world's most notorious atheist changed his mind.* New York: HarperCollins, 2007.

Ford, Norman M. *When did I begin?* Cambridge: Cambridge University Press, 1991.

Frankl, Viktor E. *Man's Search for Meaning.* New York: Washington Square Press, 1984.

Harris, Sam. *The End of Faith: Religion, Terror, and the Future of Reason.* New York: W.W. Norton, 2004.

Hawking, Stephen. *A Brief of History of Time.* New York: Bantam Books, 1990.

Herrick, Paul. *The Many Worlds of Logic.* Fort Worth: Harcourt Brace, 2000.

Hoffman, Albert. *LSD: My Problem Child,* translated by J. Ott. Sarasota, Florida: Multidisciplinary Association for Psychedelic Studies, 2005.

James, William. 'The Dilemma of Determinism,' An address to the Harvard Divinity Students published in the *Unitarian Review,* 1884 (also available in Kolak and Martin).

_____. *Pragmatism and Other Writings.* New York: Penguin Books, 2000.

Jung, C. G. *Synchronicity: An Acausal Connecting Principle.* Princeton: Princeton University Press, 1973.

Kafka, Franz. *Metamorphosis.* West Valley City, Utah: Waking Lion Press, 2006.

Kane, Robert. *The Significance of Free Will.* Oxford: Oxford

University Press, 1966.

Kauffman, Stuart A. *Reinventing the Sacred*. New York: Basic Books, 2008.

Kierkegaard, Soren. *Fear and Trembling*, translated by A. Hannay. London: Penguin Books, 2003.

Klinghoffer, David. *Why the Jews Rejected Jesus*. New York: Three Leaves Press, 2005.

Kolak, Daniel and Martin, Raymond, *The Experience of Philosophy*, 5th ed. Belmont, California: Wadsworth/Thomson Learning, 2002.

Lewis, C.S. *Mere Christianity*. San Francisco: HarperCollins, 2001.

Locke, John. *A Letter Concerning Toleration*. Amherst, New York: Prometheus Books, 1990.

Marx, K. and Engels, F. "Introduction to a Critique of Hegelian Philosophy of Right," in *Collected Works*. London: Lawrence & Wishart, 1975.

Meinhardt, Molly Dewsnap, editor. *Jesus: The Last Day*. Washington, D.C.: Biblical Archaeology Society, 2003.

Miles, Jack. *Christ: A Crisis in the Life of God*. New York: Vintage Books, 2001.

_____. *God: A Biography*. New York: Vintage Books, 1995.

Miller, Kenneth R. *Finding Darwin's God: A Scientist's Search for Common Ground Between God and Evolution*. New York: Harper Perennial, 2002.

Mills, David. *Atheist Universe: The Thinking Person's Answer to Christian Fundamentalism*. Berkeley, California: Ulysses Press, 2006.

Murdoch, Iris. *Existentialists and Mystics: Writings on Philosophy and Literature*. New York: Penguin Books, 1999.

Otto, Rudolf. *The Idea of the Holy*, translated by John W. Harvey. London: Oxford University Press, 1958.

Patterson, Stephen; Borg, Marcus and Crossan, John Dominic. *The Search for Jesus: Modern Scholarship Looks at the Gospels*, edited by Hershel Shanks. Washington, D.C.: Biblical Archaeology

Society, 1994.

Popper, Karl R. "On the Status of Science and Metaphysics," in *Conjectures and Refutations: The Growth of Scientific Knowledge*. London: Routledge, 1989.

Proust, Marcel. *In Search of Lost Time*, translated by C.K. Scott Moncrieff and Terence Kilmartin, revised by D.J. Enright. New York: The Modern Library, 2004.

Rice, Anne. *Christ the Lord: Out of Egypt*. New York: Ballantine Books, 2006.

Robinson, James M., ed., *The Nag Hammadi Library in English*. San Francisco: HarperCollins, 1990.

Rupp, E.G. and Watson, P.S., translators and editors. *Luther and Erasmus: Free Will and Salvation*. Philadelphia: The Westminster Press, 1969.

Saint Augustine, *Enchiridion*, trans. J.F. Shaw, from The Works of Aurelius Augustine, vol. IX, Rev. Marcus Dods, ed., Edinburgh: T. & T. Clark, 1892, Chs. XI-XII (reprinted in Denise, White and Peterfreund).

Santayana, George. *Skepticism and Animal Faith*. New York: Dover Publications, 1955.

_____. *The Sense of Beauty*. New York: Dover Publications, 1955.

Schweitzer, Albert. *The Quest of the Historical Jesus*, trans. W. Montgomery. Mineola, New York: Dover Publications, Inc., 2005.

Searle, John R. *The Construction of Social Reality*. New York: The Free Press, 1995.

_____. *Mind: A Brief Introduction*. New York and Oxford: Oxford University Press, 2004.

_____. *Mind, Language and Society*. New York: Basic Books, 1999.

_____. *The Mystery of Consciousness*. New York: The New York Review of Books, 1997.

Segal, Jerome M. *Joseph's Bones: Understanding the Struggle Between*

God and Mankind in the Bible. New York: Riverhead Books, 2007.

Smith, Huston. *The World's Religions: Our Great Wisdom Traditions*. New York: HarperCollins, 1991.

_____. *Why Religion Matters: The Fate of the Human Spirit in an Age of Disbelief*. New York: HarperCollins, 2001.

Smullyan, Raymond M. *The Tao Is Silent*. New York: HarperCollins, 1992.

Spong, John Shelby. *A New Christianity for a New World*. New York: HarperCollins, 2002.

Stove, David. *Darwinian Fairytales: Selfish Genes, Errors of Heredity, and Other Fables of Evolution*. New York: Encounter Books, 2006.

Tabor, James D. *The Jesus Dynasty: The Hidden History of Jesus, His Royal Family, and the Birth of Christianity*. New York: Simon and Schuster, 2006.

Tillich, Paul. *The Courage to Be*, 2nd edition. New Haven and London: Yale University Press, 2000.

Weber, Max. *The Protestant Ethic and the "Spirit" of Capitalism and Other Writings*. New York: Penguin Books, 2002.

Westphal, Jonathan. 'A new way with the Consequence Argument and the fixity of the laws.' *Analysis* 63: 208-212, July 2003.

BOOKS

O is a symbol of the world, of oneness and unity. In different cultures it also means the "eye," symbolizing knowledge and insight. We aim to publish books that are accessible, constructive and that challenge accepted opinion, both that of academia and the "moral majority."

Our books are available in all good English language bookstores worldwide. If you don't see the book on the shelves ask the bookstore to order it for you, quoting the ISBN number and title. Alternatively you can order online (all major online retail sites carry our titles) or contact the distributor in the relevant country, listed on the copyright page.

See our website **www.o-books.net** for a full list of over 500 titles, growing by 100 a year.

And tune in to myspiritradio.com for our book review radio show, hosted by June-Elleni Laine, where you can listen to the authors discussing their books.

mySpiritRadio